The
Pictorial History of the
CIVIL
WAR

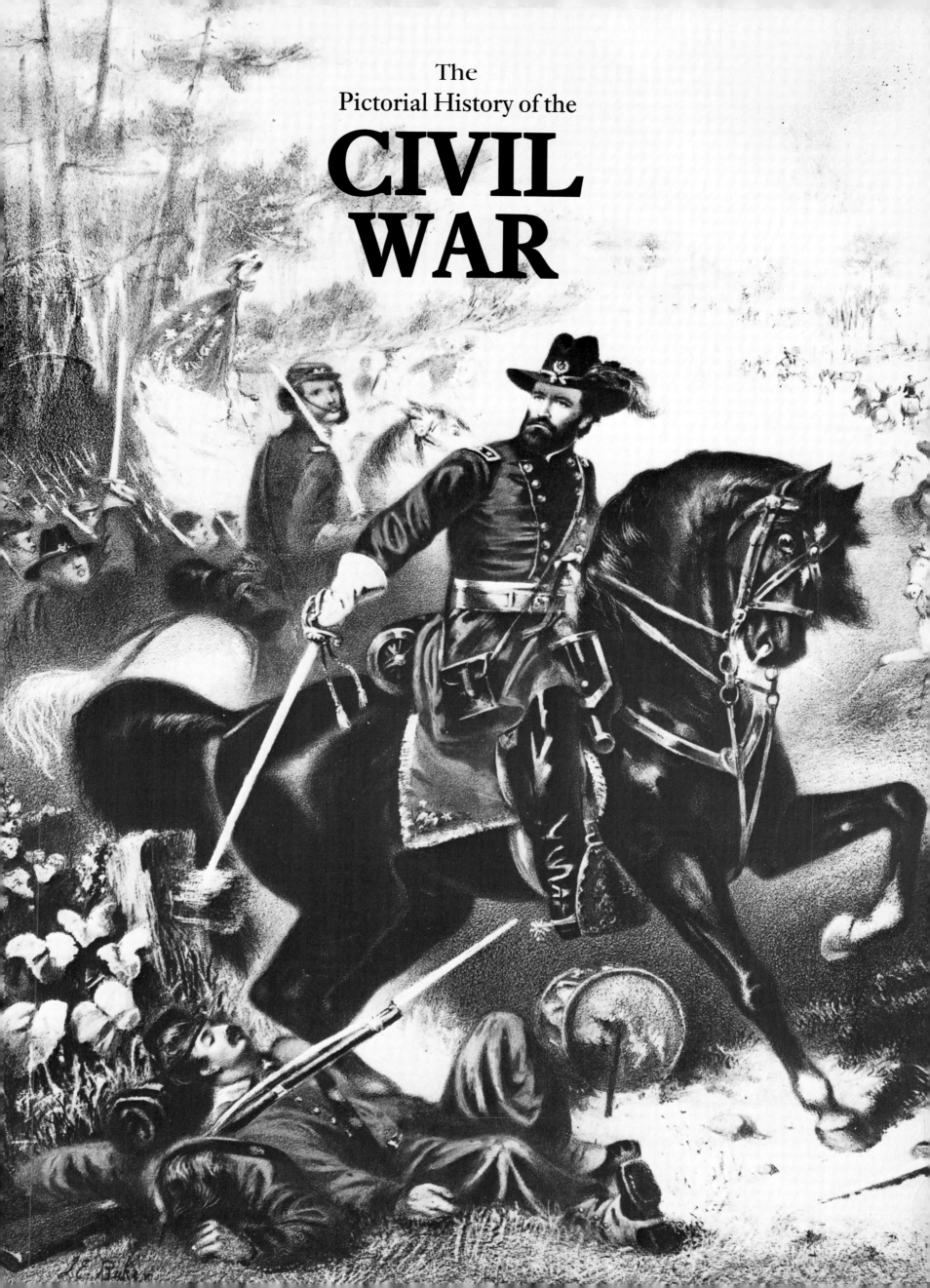

The Pictorial History of the
CIVIL WAR

Jeremy Barnes

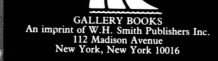

GALLERY BOOKS
An imprint of W.H. Smith Publishers Inc.
112 Madison Avenue
New York, New York 10016

Published by Gallery Books
A Division of W H Smith Publishers Inc
112 Madison Avenue
New York, New York 10016

Produced by
Brompton Books Corp.
15 Sherwood Place
Greenwich, CT 06830

ISBN 0-8317-6896-7

Printed in Spain

10 9 8 7 6 5 4 3 2

Page 1: *Ulysses S Grant.*

Page 2-3: *Union artillery is rushed up to the firing line at the height of the Battle of Gettysburg, July 1863.*

Pages 4-5: *The Battle of Shiloh.*

Contents

PART 1
The Coming of War

The Background of the War

In 1860 the American experiment was on the verge of falling apart. The nation that had considered itself an exemplar for all mankind, the chosen land of God, was gathering its arms and its enmities for a civil war. What could have brought to this point a country that had begun with such hope and conviction?

Ultimately, most wars are irrational: the forces that impel men to throw away their lives and fortunes are compounded primarily of greed, power drives, and dark passions left over from the ages before civilization. But ideological conflicts may also precipitate violence, and in the case of the United States, those conflicts surged around one issue. In 1860 the Southern states of the nation were the last in the Western world to maintain the institution of human slavery.

The Dutch had first brought black slaves to America in the early 17th century; by the time of the Revolution, there were half a million in the country. But the contradiction of slavery

Previous pages: *A battery of Union horse artillery goes into action in support of an advancing cavalry regiment.*

Above: *Statesman John C Calhoun, who played an important role in American politics from the War of 1812 until 1850. A native of South Carolina, he helped shape the theories of states' rights and nullification – moving forces behind the South's effort to achieve national independence in the Civil War. The daguerrotype (c 1849) is by pioneer photographer Mathew B Brady.*

Left: *Sugar cane, a labor-intensive crop, is cut and weeded by slaves on a Louisiana plantation.*

Right: *Frontispiece for Harriet Beecher Stowe's* Uncle Tom's Cabin, *published in Boston in 1852.*

Above: *William Lloyd Garrison, editor of* The Liberator, *the influential abolitionist newspaper. He published it in Boston from 1831 until 1865, when the Thirteenth Amendment to the Constitution ended slavery.*

Above: *An 1850 lithograph entitled* Effects of the Fugitive Slave Law: *armed pursuers fire upon fleeing slaves. Northern abolitionists encouraged people to disobey federal laws demanding the return of such fugitives.*

and the American idea was too manifest to be ignored forever. In the Declaration of Independence, the first sentence proclaimed that 'all men are created equal.' America was the first country in history to erect that principle as the foundation of a state. At the same time, by tolerating slavery it maintained the most galling denial of that principle, creating a deep flaw at its very foundation. The resulting instability troubled the founding fathers. Thomas Jefferson said, 'I tremble for my country' at the thought of what slavery was leading to. (Yet Jefferson himself owned slaves: like most Southern planters, he could not imagine any other way of working his land.)

Unwittingly, Jefferson provided the ideological basis that extended the life of slavery – the concept of states' rights. He saw the primacy of state governments over the national as a bastion of democracy. During the 19th century, that idea would be taken up by political theorists like South Carolinian John C. Calhoun and made into the rationale for protecting slavery: it was a matter for each state to decide, and the federal government had no right to interfere. Moreover, if the national government passed any law objectionable to a state, that state had the right to nullify it – or to secede from the Union if federal interference went too far.

The moral and legal tensions around slavery grew steadily during the 19th century. Beginning with the Quakers around the time of the Revolution, an abolitionist movement grew up. Slavery was abolished in New England and the Middle Atlantic states in the later 18th century. Congress began to chip away at the institution, forbidding the overseas slave trade in 1808. A series of Congressional compromises – which satisfied no one fully – protected slavery in the South but placed some barriers to its spread into new territories. Meanwhile, the slave population of the South increased to over four million by 1860; slavery was the indispensable foundation of the region's agrarian, cotton-based economy. And the South became steadily more defiant in the defense of its institutions and its culture. The plantation aristocracy took to calling themselves 'Southrens'; they viewed their society as separate from that of the North, a chivalrous milieu of bold cavaliers and noble ladies. As the uncompromising sectionalism of the South grew, so did antislavery sentiment in the North – and the fulminations of influential abolitionists like William Lloyd Garrison.

Left: Radical abolitionist John Brown and his followers hold federal hostages in the arsenal at Harpers Ferry during their 1859 raid. The insurrection was quelled by government troops led by Colonel Robert E Lee.

Right: *John Brown is led to his execution in this 1884 painting by Thomas Hovenden entitled* The Last Moments of John Brown.

Below: *The Underground Railroad, painted by Charles T Webber in 1893. The network of Northern abolitionists and Southern blacks who helped fugitive slaves escape to freedom became part of American history between 1830 and 1860.*

Stowe's book was part of a web of events that led inexorably toward war. It followed by two years the Fugitive Slave Act, which alarmed antislavery forces by mandating stringent penalties for helping slaves to escape (by then Northern abolitionists were bringing out a stream of fugitives by way of the 'Underground Railroad'). In 1857 came the deplorable Dred Scott decision by the conservative Supreme Court, which defined slaves as mere property, having no rights of citizenship. In the mid-1850s, violence raged in the territory of Kansas between pro- and antislavery factions, and the news from 'Bleeding Kansas' was a source of national anxiety. Finally, and most ominously of all, came the spectre of the South's greatest fear, that of a slave revolt. In October 1859, the fanatical abolitionist John Brown led an armed group of blacks and whites in an attempt to seize the federal arsenal at Harpers Ferry, Virginia (now West Virginia), to prepare an impossible plan for a general uprising of slaves. Brown was quickly captured and hanged, but his action broke over the country like a thunderclap. By then, a new political party – the Republicans – had formed, the first to oppose slavery explicitly.

Abraham Lincoln

As a politician, Abraham Lincoln was not averse to letting his humble background be made known by his supporters. Some of the stories were even true – he was, in fact, born in a log cabin in Kentucky and spent an impoverished childhood farming with his father in Indiana. As president, however, he confessed that his reputation as a rail-splitter was imaginary; he could hardly remember spending a day at that job.

Less widely known was how much Lincoln had hated poverty and life on the farm. In his youth he formed an intense determination to get somewhere in the world; it was ambition as much as intellectual curiosity that led him, in the absence of formal schooling, to educate himself to the point where he became one of the greatest writers in the history of politics. His gift for language was one source of his greatness, rather than his oratory itself, which was flawed by his high, unimpressive voice and ungainly physique.

Lincoln studied law and settled into practice in Springfield, Illinois. He married well, prospered in his practice, moved into state politics as a Whig, and served one unpromising term in the U.S. House of Representatives in the late 1840s. Failing to win re-election, he was ready to quit politics when the slavery issue began to boil over, and he trained the power of his rhetoric on the pressing issue of the day. In 1854 he spoke against Illinois

Democratic senator Stephen A Douglas, who supported the pending Kansas-Nebraska Bill, which would allow those territories to vote for or against slavery rather than having the government forbid it outright. In 1858, now a Republican, Lincoln took part in a historic series of debates with Douglas in a contest for his seat in the Senate. Douglas won re-election, but during the debates Lincoln kindled antislavery sentiment across the nation, saying, 'A house divided against itself cannot stand.' Two years and many riveting speeches later, he became the Republican nominee for president.

Because the Democrats had split along sectional lines, each faction running a candidate (one of whom was the compromising Douglas), Lincoln won the election. Although deeply against slavery personally, he had presented himself as a moderate, proposing not to interfere with slavery in the South, but to prohibit it in new territories that sought statehood. For the South, however, that compromise was not acceptable: some states had threatened to secede from the Union if the Republican candidate were elected, and they were prepared to make good on that threat. Thus it would fall to Abraham Lincoln, who had held national office for only two years, and that unsuccessfully, to try and keep the United States together.

Top left and right: *Abraham Lincoln in 1859, the year before he became the Republican candidate for president, and in 1864, visibly aged by the Civil War.*

Above: *Illinois attorney Stephen A Douglas, who championed the principle of popular sovereignty in the slavery debate and defeated Abraham Lincoln in the 1858 race for the Senate. Nominated for president in 1860 by Northern Democrats, Douglas was rejected by the South.*

Left: *The Lincoln-Douglas debates on the issue of slavery and its extension attracted national attention in 1858.*

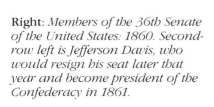

Right: *Members of the 36th Senate of the United States: 1860. Second-row left is Jefferson Davis, who would resign his seat later that year and become president of the Confederacy in 1861.*

Secession

The long-expected, long-feared step was taken by a South Carolina convention on 20 December 1860, two weeks after Lincoln's election. The ordinance read: 'We, the people of the State of South Carolina . . . do declare and ordain . . . that the union now subsiding between South Carolina and other States under the name of the United States of America is hereby dissolved.' By the time Lincoln was inaugurated on 4 March, seven states had seceded and formed the Confederate States of America: South Carolina, Mississippi, Florida, Alabama, Georgia, Louisiana, and Texas. The new country already had a provisional government, a provisional constitution protecting slavery, and a provisional president – Jefferson Davis, former Congressman, Senator, and Secretary of War.

As he would do so many times, Lincoln, in his inaugural address, walked a tightrope of fine legal and political distinctions. 'I have no purpose . . . to interfere with the institution of slavery,' he said; however, 'No state, on its own mere action, can get out of the Union.' He thereby defined the conflict as one over secession, which was illegal, and not over Southern slavery, which remained legal. Thus if war came, it would be the South's doing: 'In *your* hands, my dissatisfied fellow countrymen, and not in *mine*, is the momentous issue of civil war.' He finished with an unforgettable peroration: 'We are not enemies, but friends. We must not be enemies. Though passion may have strained, it must not break, our bonds of affection. The mystic chords of memory . . . will yet swell the chorus of the Union when again touched, as surely they will be, by the better angels of our nature.'

In the weeks that followed, Lincoln prepared to make a stand at Fort Sumter, which stood ringed by Confederate cannon in Charleston Harbor, South Carolina. The better angels had failed.

CHARLESTON MERCURY

EXTRA:

Passed unanimously at 1.15 o'clock, P. M. December 20th, 1860.

AN ORDINANCE

To dissolve the Union between the State of South Carolina and other States united with her under the compact entitled " The Constitution of the United States of America."

We, the People of the State of South Carolina, in Convention assembled, do declare and ordain, and it is hereby declared and ordained,

That the Ordinance adopted by us in Convention, on the twenty-third day of May, in the year of our Lord one thousand seven hundred and eighty-eight, whereby the Constitution of the United States of America was ratified, and also, all Acts and parts of Acts of the General Assembly of this State, ratifying amendments of the said Constitution, are hereby repealed; and that the union now subsisting between South Carolina and other States, under the name of " The United States of America," is hereby dissolved.

THE UNION IS DISSOLVED!

Above: *The special edition of the* Charleston Mercury *that announced South Carolina's secession from the Union on 20 December 1860.*

Left: *Jefferson Davis's inauguration as president of the Confederate States of America at Montgomery, Alabama's state capital.*

Right: *The pre-Civil War volunteer movement in the North, as satirized by* Harper's Weekly *in the fall of 1860. The sketch is entitled* Training Day in the Country.

Left: *The bombardment of Fort Sumter in Charleston Harbor, 12–13 April 1861, as depicted by Currier & Ives.*

Above: *Confederate General Pierre G T Beauregard, who came from a distinguished Louisiana Creole family, became the South's first war hero when he captured Fort Sumter.*

Top: *Encircled by Confederate batteries, the Federal garrison inside Fort Sumter never had a chance of repelling the Southern attack.*

Right: *Major Robert Anderson, who commanded Fort Sumter, was promoted to brigadier general in recognition of his role in the war's first engagement.*

Then a Federal gunner was surprised to see a face appear before his gun embrasure; it was the former Senator Wigfall of Texas, who had come out on his own tack to accept the fort's surrender. Wigfall was hauled in before he could be killed by fire from his own side. The official delegation arrived soon afterward, and some confused negotiations ensued. There was no doubt about the surrender, however; the fort had taken 4000 shells in 34 hours of nearly continuous bombardment, and the Federals had little ammunition left. Finally, terms were agreed upon: the Federals would depart next day after saluting their flag with cannon.

At that point there had been no casualties on either side. But as Anderson's men fired their salute on 14 April, some sparks from the smoldering fire in the fort touched off a paper cannon cartridge as it was being loaded. The explosion claimed the first life of the war, Private Daniel Hough, and wounded five others, one of whom soon died. Then, with the band playing 'Yankee Doodle' and Southerners cheering from the shore, the Northern men boarded a boat for New York, and Confederate soldiers marched into Fort Sumter. It all seemed a rather gentlemanly affair.

A silk flag donated by the ladies of Charleston was run up the flagpole. Despite subsequent Union attempts to recapture Fort Sumter, the flag of the South would not come down until the end of the war: the fort was destined to remain a powerful symbol of Southern resistance. Shortly after the fall of Fort Sumter, four more states joined the Confederacy – Virginia, Arkansas, Tennessee, and North Carolina.

Above: A contemporary painting of the city of Charleston and its harbor at the outbreak of the Civil War by Conrad Wise Chapman.

Left: Chapman's 1863 painting of the brick fortress of Fort Sumter, three miles out from Charleston.

Right: The Confederate flag over Fort Sumter would be the target of Union guns throughout the war, but it continued to fly until 1865.

Washington Prepares to Fight

When Sumter fell, Lincoln faced a host of difficult decisions. He had to respond firmly and yet leave the door open to peace and he had to organize a war without impinging too much upon the authority of Congress, which was then in recess. Most of all, he had to avoid alienating the border states of Missouri, Maryland, Kentucky, and Delaware; although the first three were slave-holding states, all were leaning slightly toward the Union. If those states went to the Confederacy, it would tip the balance disastrously, so Lincoln proceeded carefully. He declared, not a war, but a state of 'insurrection' and called for 75,000 volunteers for three months' service. He also ordered a blockade of all ports within the Confederacy and, most controversially, suspended the writ of habeas corpus in an area stretching from Philadelphia to Washington, mainly to contain pro-Southern rioting that had been raging in Baltimore. In early May, he called for 42,000 more Army volunteers and 18,000 seamen.

The Union had no unified strategy for pursuing the war and would have none for months to come. The first engagements were small, sporadic, and practically accidental. On 18 May 1861, Federal units engaged Confederate batteries at Sewall's Point, Virginia. Six days later Federal troops occupied Alexandria, Virginia, with little resistance, in order to help protect Washington. Elmer Ellsworth, head of the Eleventh New York Regiment, was fatally shot by a hotel keeper as he tried to remove a Confederate flag from the hotel roof, and a Union soldier killed the assailant. In early June there was fighting in northern Virginia, and Union forces sent Confederates running in western Virginia. The latter event encouraged Union loyalists to form a pro-Union government of West Virginia, permanently dividing the state.

With each engagement, casualties escalated. In mid-June defeated Federal forces at Bethel Church, Virginia, lost 18 dead and 53 wounded. A month later, Union general George B McClellan became the North's first war hero when he crushed Confederate forces in West Virginia to secure the new pro-Union government. Then the first big battle exploded and set the course of the war for months to come.

Left: *A recruiting poster for the Fourth New Hampshire Regiment, offering a $10 bounty in addition to Regular Army pay and rations: September 1861.*

Top: *The Union recruiting office in Boston.*

Above: *Confederate troops entrain for Manassas on the eve of the war's first great battle – Bull Run.*

Top right: *Jefferson Davis (seated at table, left) and his cabinet, including General Robert E Lee (center).*

Right: *Recruiting troops for the Confederate Army at Woodstock. Virginia: Harper's Weekly, 5 October 1861.*

The First Battle of Bull Run

On both sides, volunteers young and old flocked to the colors, fired by dreams of patriotic glory and romantic battle. We see them in old photographs: men sitting stiffly and proudly for the slow cameras of the day in their new blue or gray uniforms, some brandishing rifles, some with knives and defiant grins. Their faces show both excitement and innocence. Most of these aspiring soldiers had only hazy ideas of what the war was about. The young Southerners tended to think they were fighting to keep invading Yankees from their hearths and homes; few Northern soldiers cared one way or another about slavery, but they were ready to fight to preserve the Union. Most men of both sides had pursued drab labor on farms or in the cities. The war was the first truly thrilling event of their lives, although they would acquire a terrible education in the realities of armed conflict in the years ahead.

The officers of both sides were largely members of the small club of West Point graduates. They had fought together in the Mexican War; they were old friends. Among those who went over to the South was Colonel Robert E Lee, son of Revolutionary War hero 'Light Horse Harry' Lee. He had been the star of his class at the Point and was considered by many the best man in the US Army. In his letter of resignation he declared that he could not raise his hand against his beloved state of Virginia. Confederate president Jefferson Davis immediately made Lee a general and gave him command of operations in his home state.

Left: *General Irvin McDowell, the first leader of the Union Army of the Potomac, lost his command after the defeat at First Bull Run.*

Above: *General George Brinton McClellan commanded the Department of Ohio before he was given McDowell's former command in the Eastern theater. When the aged Winfield Scott retired as general-in-chief of the army, McClellan received this top position as well.*

Top right: *The 25 generals of the Confederate Army with Robert E Lee, commander of the Army of Northern Virginia, in 1862.*

Right: *Commander Winfield Scott (center) and officers in Mexico.*

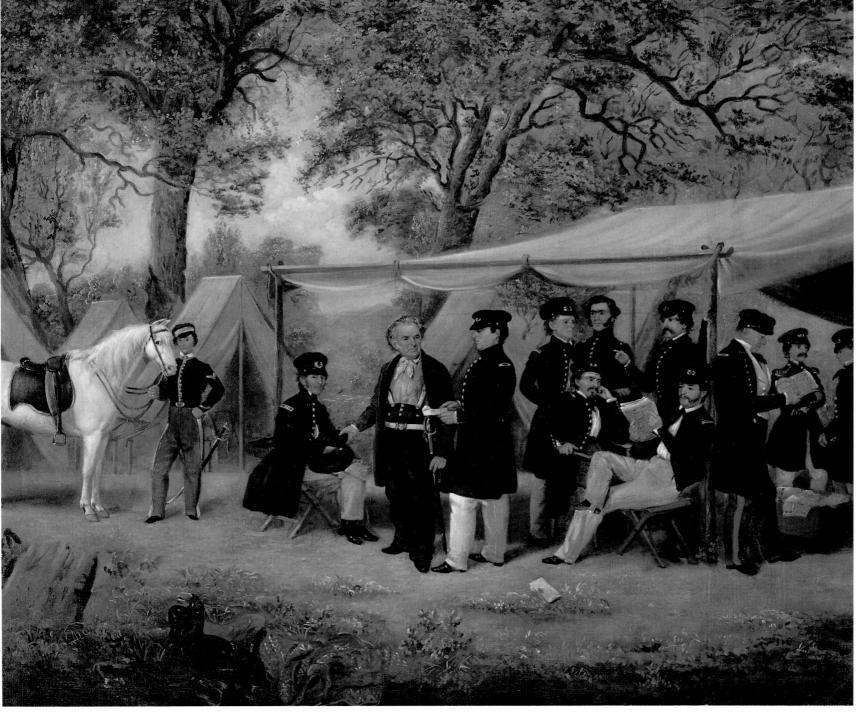

In July 1861, Southern general P G T Beauregard commanded a force of 22,000 men encamped at Manassas Junction, Virginia, some 25 miles southwest of Washington. Lincoln ordered General Irvin McDowell to drive Beauregard away from that important rail junction. On the 16th, McDowell advanced with 30,600 troops, primarily three-month volunteers and militia. Having learned of the advance from spies in Washington, Beauregard called for reinforcements, and President Davis ordered General Joseph E Johnston to bring his 11,000 men by railroad from Virginia's Shenandoah Valley (this was the first large movement of troops by rail in history). Everyone knew a big battle was coming; most hoped it would decide the matter once and for all. (As the Union generally named battles for the nearest stream, it would call this one Bull Run. The South would call it Manassas, for the nearby town.)

The forces collided briefly in a skirmish at Blackburn's Ford, where General James Longstreet drove away a Federal reconnaissance party. McDowell was hesitant, unsure of his green troops, and his delay in attacking allowed time for Johnston's reinforcements to arrive, giving Beauregard a force of well over 30,000. Beauregard and McDowell had been classmates at West Point, and they made identical plans for battle – feint with the left, attack with the right. If both had been successful, the two armies might have brushed past each other like a swinging door, the Confederates heading for Washington and the Federals for the new Southern capital of Richmond. In practice, however, the battle was a free-for-all.

On 21 July, McDowell set his plan in motion and got the jump on Beauregard. The plan then fell apart, due largely to the inexperience of the Federal troops. It took a great deal of practice for an army of that era to move on a battlefield; even the simple matter of getting from a marching column into line of battle was something that had to be drilled until it was automatic, or the troops would never manage it when bullets and shells were flying. Thus McDowell made his feint on the Southern right effectively, followed by a secondary attack on the enemy center. But to mount his main attack on the left, he had to march his men 15 miles through rough terrain. By the time McDowell had struggled to the Confederate left, Beauregard had been alerted and had shifted troops there.

The two forces collided at Henry House Hill, and the Southerners began to fall back. But then brigade commander Thomas J Jackson formed his troops into a defensive nucleus on the hilltop. In his last moments of life, Southern general Bernard E Bee entered history, shouting to his men 'Look at Jackson's Brigade – it stands like a stone wall! Rally behind the Virginians!' In short order, the Confederate line had firmed up behind Jackson, and he led a counterattack that pushed back the Union right. It was in those moments that the laconic, eccentric brigade commander came to be called Stonewall Jackson, his troops, the Stonewall Brigade.

At dusk the Federals began an orderly retreat, with no Confederate pursuit. Among the column were a number of civilians who had come to watch the battle, bringing picnic lunches. Suddenly, a Southern battery fired some shells into the mass of soldiers and civilians near a bridge over Bull Run that constricted the column. There was an instant panic, and the retreat became rout and chaos. The South had won its first major victory.

That night all Washington learned of the disaster when the troops that had marched grandly off to battle staggered back into the city, a ragged, demoralized rabble. The North was horrified, and none more so than the man on whose shoulders the war now rested. Poet Walt Whitman, who lived in Washington and chronicled the war there, would write of the president on that terrible day, 'If there were nothing else of Abraham Lincoln for history to stamp him with, it is enough . . . that he endured that hour, that day, bitterer than gall – indeed a crucifixion day . . . and resolv'd to lift himself and the Union out of it.'

Top: *Brigade commander Thomas J Jackson at the First Battle of Bull Run (Manassas), where he earned the nickname 'Stonewall' for the firmness with which he stood his ground.*

Above: *Confederate fortifications around Manassas, Virginia, in July 1861.*

Top right: *Civil War artist Alfred R Waud sketched General McClellan and the 5th Cavalry crossing Bull Run at Blackburn's Ford.*

Right: *Union and Confederate troops clash on a bridge before the Union retreat from Manassas to Washington, DC. Opposing forces at First Bull Run were composed mainly of poorly trained volunteers, but the South won the day.*

Above: *General Ambrose E Burnside and his brigade of Rhode Island volunteers at First Bull Run. Burnside's early Civil War career saw some notable successes, but his abortive assault on Richmond in 1862 was the beginning of a disastrous decline.*

Left: *Union Colonel Michael Corcoran leads the 'Gallant Sixty-ninth' in a costly assault on Confederate batteries at First Bull Run.*

Right: *The Confederate Black Horse Cavalry falls to a charge by Union Zouaves, whose colorful uniforms were patterned after those of Algerian units in the French Army.*

Following pages: *The Battle of Perryville, Kentucky, October 1862.*

PART 2
The Realities of War

McClellan Builds an Army

When the war began, many of the best officers of the regular army went to the South – men like Lee, J E Johnston, and Beauregard. By contrast, the North faced a crisis of leadership. The Army's General in Chief at the outset was the aged and creaky Winfield Scott, hero of the War of 1812, who was generally known as 'Old Fuss and Feathers.' Lincoln knew he had to find younger and more dynamic leadership. After General McDowell's rout at Bull Run, the president fixed on a young general of 34 who had been celebrated for his operations in West Virginia – General George Brinton McClellan.

In July 1861, Lincoln gave McClellan command of the Federal Division of the Potomac; his assignment was to rebuild the defeated forces of Bull Run into an army that could conquer Virginia. With the full resources of the federal government behind

Left: *The personable and handsome George B McClellan was venerated by his men, but he lacked the decisiveness essential to a commander.*

Above: *General Winfield Scott, a hero of the War of 1812, was 75 years old when the Civil War broke out. He had served as general-in-chief of the US Army since 1841.*

Right: *Scott had warned that war was imminent soon after Lincoln's election, and he took steps to recruit and train an army for the defense of Washington before tendering his resignation. Lincoln and his cabinet extended full honors to the aged commander.*

him, McClellan set to the task with a brilliant gift for organization. So impressive were his abilities off the battlefield, so confident and authoritative his manner, that in December he was also named to replace Scott as General in Chief of the Union Army. The men of the Army of the Potomac, McClellan's creation, admired him extravagantly, calling the diminutive general 'Little Mac' and 'the Young Napoleon.'

In the end, however, Little Mac's faults would be inseparable from his virtues. His confidence boiled over into arrogance; his high-handed treatment of the president would verge on insubordination. Worse, his elaborate caution and protective attitude toward his men would make him slow-moving and indecisive on the battlefield. As one contemporary wrote of McClellan, 'Though no commander ever had the love of his soldiers more, or tried more to spare their lives, [he] never realized the metal that was in his grand Army of the Potomac.'

The Battle of Logan Cross Roads

The border states of Kentucky, Maryland, Missouri, and Delaware would finally remain with the Union, but first the South made major efforts to claim them – efforts that were supported by many of the states' citizens. In late 1861 and into January, Union and Confederate forces had been maneuvering in Kentucky. Finally, Federal forces under General George H Thomas closed in on Confederates at Mill Springs, on the Cumberland River.

The Battle of Logan Cross Roads (or Mill Springs) broke out when General George B Crittenden's troops attacked a detachment of Thomas's at midnight, in driving rain, on 19 January 1862. The darkness and bad weather quickly led to a setback for the South: General Felix Zollicoffer, commanding two Confederate regiments, came across a Union officer and began giving him orders, under the impression that he was a subordinate; in the process, Zollicoffer was shot and killed. Crittenden determinedly reorganized his forces for an assault, as Thomas arrived on the scene to take charge on the Union side.

In fierce fighting, Thomas's men broke the Confederate left and started a rout. Most of the Confederates escaped, but many deserted – Southern losses were 125 killed, 309 wounded, 99 missing. Union casualties were 39 killed, 207 wounded, 15 captured. The defeat at Logan Cross Roads created a critical gap in the Confederate line of defense in the Tennessee-Kentucky area, a strategic weakness that was soon to benefit a then unknown Yankee general named Ulysses S Grant.

Near right: *A Confederate sharpshooter takes aim from his perch in a tree.*

Far right: *Southern families flee their homes as a battle impends.*

Below: *A Confederate officer made this sketch of a Southern battery drawn to the battlefield by oxen.*

A Confederate Batt

altery previous to the Battle of Bull-Run.

Grant Takes Forts Henry and Donelson

In February 1862, a Union force gathered to mount an attack on Fort Henry, a Confederate garrison on the Tennessee River. The operation was intended to be the first step in gaining a Union foothold within the South. In command was Brigadier General Ulysses S Grant, of whom no one expected much. He had been an undistinguished West Pointer and an equally undistinguished officer in the Mexican War, after which he had drunk himself out of the servive and capped it all by failing as a farmer. When the Civil War began, he had more or less begged his way back into the army; the Union was desperate enough for generals to take him.

Grant arrived outside Fort Henry on 6 February to find that the enemy commander had sent most of the garrison overland to reinforce the more important Fort Donelson, on the Cumberland River in northwestern Tennessee. Only 100 artillerymen were left in Fort Henry, which moreover was unfinished and partly flooded. Since Grant had 15,000 men and 7 gunboats, the result was never in question: the Rebels in Fort Henry surrendered in short order. Grant then headed for Fort Donelson, a much more formidable objective.

Top: *General Grant's army launches its assault on Fort Donelson, Tennessee.*

Above: *The evacuation of the Cumberland Gap in the wake of Grant's victory at Fort Donelson, on the Cumberland River, in February 1862. Confederate loss of control over the Tennessee and Cumberland Rivers made the South vulnerable to invasion.*

Left: *Confederate General Simon Bolivar Buckner and his force of 7000 had to give up Fort Donelson under Grant's terms of 'unconditional surrender.' It was the first decisive Union victory of the war.*

FREEMEN!
AVOID CONSCRIPTION!

The undersigned desires to raise a Company for the Confederate States service, and for that purpose I call upon the people of the Counties of Jefferson and Hawkins, Tenn., to meet promptly at Russellville, on SATURDAY, JULY 19th, 1862, and organize a Company.

By so doing you will avoid being taken as Conscripts, for that Act will now be enforced by order of the War Department. Rally, then, my Countrymen, to your Country's call.

S. M. DENNISON,
Of the Confederate States Army.

CHARLESTON, Tenn., JUNE 30, 1862.

Bottom left: *During the second year of the war, the Confederacy enacted a draft of all able-bodied freemen between the ages of 18 and 35. At this time, the South had 29 percent of the nation's population while the North had 71 percent.*

Below: *Four Union ironclads and several wooden vessels took part in the attack on Fort Donelson. Two of the ironclads,* St. Louis *and* Louisville, *were disabled by Confederate shore batteries.*

With the 27,000 troops now under his command, Grant besieged Donelson on 13 February 1862. Inside were some 21,000 Confederates – divisions led by Gideon J Pillow and Simon Bolivar Buckner under overall command of General John Floyd. That night a roaring blizzard and subzero temperatures set in; the bluecoats had to sleep outside in the miserable weather. Grant's gunboats arrived on the 14th to shell the fort, but Donelson's batteries managed to drive them off. Next morning, the Confederates emerged to assault the surrounding Federals; with Colonel Nathan Bedford Forrest spearheading the attack, they opened up a potential escape route toward the east. At that point, Grant was away conferring with his gunboat commander.

However, the Confederates then succumbed to indecisiveness. As Buckner and Pillow wrangled about whether to abandon the fort and march to Nashville or to continue the attack, Floyd decided to do neither. Instead, he called all his troops back into the fort, losing the advantage he had gained. By then, Grant had arrived on the field, nearly surrounded the fort with his men, and begun closing off the escape route. On the night of

15 February, Floyd passed command to General Buckner and escaped with Pillow, Forrest, and some 3000 troops. It was assumed that Buckner, who was an old friend of Grant's, could get more favorable terms of surrender. But Grant quickly disabused his friend of that idea. When Buckner requested terms, Grant sent the reply that made him famous: 'No terms except unconditional and immediate surrender can be accepted. I propose to move immediately upon your works. I am sir, very respectfully, Your obt. svt. U.S. Grant.' Buckner was furious, but had no choice – on the 16th he surrendered with some 7000 men. Grant had captured the better part of an entire army.

The fall of Fort Donelson was the North's first decisive victory of the war. It virtually ended Confederate hopes of conquering Kentucky and claimed much of Tennessee for the Union, including the vital Tennessee River. Now the stage was set for a vertical split of the Confederacy by a Union drive down the Mississippi River – a drive in which Grant would be a prime mover. And the rejoicing North had a hero, whose initials were the basis of a nickname by which everyone would know him: Unconditional Surrender Grant.

Fighting in Arkansas

The area west of the Mississippi River was vitally important to the Confederacy, much of whose sustenance flowed east across the river from Arkansas and Mississippi. The main focus of Union efforts was to capture the river itself, but Federal armies also operated in the Trans-Mississippi. At the end of 1861, General Sam Curtis took command of the Union Army of the Southwest. In March, Curtis's force of 11,000 men was near Pea Ridge, Arkansas, when scout James B 'Wild Bill' Hickok brought word that Confederates – 17,000 troops under General Earl Van Dorn – were advancing to the attack. Curtis put his men in defensive positions near the ridge and waited.

The Southerners arrived exhausted from a 55-mile march in wet snow; Commander Van Dorn was sick and issuing orders from an ambulance wagon. On the eve of the battle, three Indian regiments arrived to fight with the Confederates. As the battle began on the morning of 7 March, Van Dorn's troops attempted to strike Curtis's left rear while the Indians made a secondary attack; the final plan called for envelopment of Federal positions near Leetown. However, Curtis's men held all along the line, while Confederate Generals McCulloch and McIntosh were killed and the Indians fell into confusion.

Seeing that Van Dorn was preparing to attack again next day, Curtis pulled his forces into a compact line. On 8 March, he sent General Franz Sigel to strike the Confederate right; following an artillery barrage, Sigel's infantry charged into the enemy and drove them back from Pea Ridge. As that advance was making progress, Curtis attacked from his right and broke Van Dorn's line to pieces. The Confederates fled to the Arkansas River, where they were ordered to leave Arkansas and join in the defense of the Mississippi. The Battle of Pea Ridge, the most significant engagement of the war in the Trans-Mississippi, ended with a strong Union presence in Arkansas.

Left: *In a propaganda cartoon by Thomas Nast, drunken Confederate guerrillas raiding a Western town terrorize women and children, kill civilians, and plunder goods. A villainous-looking 'Rebel' shoots down a dog in the street at lower right.*

Top: *The Battle of Pea Ridge, Arkansas, 7-8 March 1862. Some 13,000 Union troops led by General Samuel Curtis defeat a much larger Confederate force and come a step closer to control of the Mississippi River.*

Above: *1862 saw heavy fighting in the Western theater, as here at Corinth, Mississippi, where Union generals John Pope, U S Grant, and Don Carlos Buell launched a successful attack in May.*

The Battle of Ironclads

At the beginning of the conflict, both sides knew that a revolutionary change in naval warfare was on the horizon – ironclad ships, which would be immensely more resistant to cannon fire than wooden vessels. The historic step toward an ironclad fleet was first taken by Confederate Secretary of the Navy Stephen R Mallory, who had to be innovative and resourceful, since the South lacked the industrial and shipbuilding capacity of the North.

The Union inadvertently contributed to Mallory's plan in April 1861: forced to abandon the Norfolk, Virginia, Navy yard, Federals failed to destroy completely the steam frigate USS *Merrimack*. The Confederates salvaged the ship with hull and engines intact and rebuilt it into the world's first completely ironclad vessel. Its main feature, extending for 170 feet of its 260-foot length, was a sloping citadel made of 22 inches of oak covered by four inches of railroad iron and crowned by a smokestack. It carried four rifled guns and six smoothbores, and an iron ramming prow projected from the front. Sailing with its armored decks awash, the ship resembled a floating barn roof with a smoking stovepipe. The ship was rechristened the CSS *Virginia*, but history has persisted in calling it the *Merrimack*.

Washington got wind of the Southern ironclad project soon after it began in 1861, and Navy Secretary Gideon Welles made haste to develop comparable armored ships for the Union. Swedish-born inventor John Ericsson had been working on the problem for some time already and his ideas were far more elaborate than the Confederates'. His design featured a hull that was flat on top and covered with iron plates, floating only a few feet above the waterline. Rising from this iron raft were a stubby pilothouse in front, a short smokestack to the rear, and in the middle a heavily armored rotating iron turret some 9 feet high and 140 tons in weight. The ship was armed with only two large smoothbore cannons, but the turret enabled them to fire in any direction. The odd-looking result, finished in January 1862, was dubbed 'Ericsson's Folly' and 'cheesebox on a raft' by skeptical observers.

The *Monitor* was ready none too soon, because on 8 March 1862 the *Merrimack* made its devastating first appearance off the coast of Virginia, at Hampton Roads, where it sailed into the middle of a Union blockading fleet. As the wooden ships frantically bombarded the ironclad, the *Merrimack* rammed the frigate *Cumberland* and shelled it as it sank. Meanwhile, accompanying Southern ships crippled the 50-gun *Congress*, and three Union steam frigates ran aground while trying to help. The battle was a nightmare for the Union commanders, who could see their cannonballs bouncing off the *Merrimack* like marbles off a brick wall. Finally in late afternoon the ironclad lumbered off with little damage – its ramming prow had

Right: *The history-making clash of the ironclads* Monitor *and* Merrimack *(CSS* Virginia) *in Hampton Roads, 9 March 1862.*

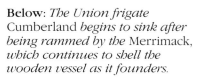

Below: *The Union frigate* Cumberland *begins to sink after being rammed by the* Merrimack, *which continues to shell the wooden vessel as it founders.*

broken off, and Captain Buchanan had been injured. Lieutenant Catesby ap Roger Jones took command. It was presumed by everyone that next day the *Merrimack* would finish off the Union fleet.

But as the Confederate ironclad steamed out to Hampton Roads on 9 March, her sailors saw a bizarre object slip around a grounded Union ship and head directly for them. At first they took it for a boiler going for repair on a raft – until commander Lieutenant Lorimer Worden ordered the *Monitor's* opening shot. The first battle of ironclads was underway.

Naval engagements throughout history had been a matter of splinters and blood on wooden decks, but not this one. The two ships closed until they were touching at times and firing at pointblank range, trying without success to find a weak spot. It was an all-out battle of apparently invulnerable iron behemoths. Several times the *Merrimack* tried to ram the smaller *Monitor*, but the Union ship easily outmaneuvered her slow-moving foe. In the first two hours of fighting, the *Monitor* took

21 hits without serious damage: sailors in the sweltering turret were threatened mainly by large screwheads that came loose and ricocheted around the chamber with every hit. The Federal firing was able to crack but not penetrate the armor of the *Merrimack*, in which 21 sailors were injured, none seriously.

Just after noon, the historic battle trailed off indecisively. Over the next few days, the *Merrimack* challenged the *Monitor* several times, but it had been decided not to risk another engagement with the Union ship – she had proved the soundness of her design and had saved the Federal fleet.

Neither ironclad ever fought again. The unseaworthy *Merrimack* had to be destroyed by the Confederates when they abandoned Norfolk in May 1862; the *Monitor* was swamped and went down in a gale off Cape Hatteras in December 1862. As the North and South began building more ironclads on the model of these prototypes, governments around the world realized that their great wooden fleets had become obsolete during the course of a single afternoon in March 1862.

Above: *Troops line the shore near Norfolk, Virginia, as the USS* Monitor *engages the* Merrimack *on the morning of 9 March. Federal blockade vessels had already suffered heavy damage the previous day, when the Confederate ironclad made its first appearance.*

Left: *Union commanders were dismayed to find that their cannonballs barely made a dent in their heavily armored opponent.*

Top right: *The* Monitor's *basic design was that of a raft of iron plating surmounted by a rotating turret containing heavy guns.*

Right: *Raymond Baylees' painting* The Ironclads.

Stonewall Jackson's Shenandoah Valley Campaign

In March 1862, General McClellan pulled his Army of the Potomac out of Washington and headed for Virginia. The objective of this Peninsular Campaign was to march into Richmond, capital of the Confederacy. President Davis knew that McClellan had the strength to do that unless extraordinary measures were taken. A major part of the Confederate response was a diversionary campaign in the Shenandoah, assigned to General Thomas J 'Stonewall' Jackson, who was already in the valley with his Stonewall Brigade.

Virginia's Shenandoah Valley was critically important to the Confederacy – its fertile fields made it the South's breadbasket, and it was the ideal route for Confederate armies marching north. Because of its strategic importance, the Union had sent General Nathaniel Banks to the valley; in March 1862, Banks chased Jackson's men from Winchester and occupied the town, along with nearby Strasburg. From there Banks planned to march east to join McClellan's campaign. It was Jackson's job to keep Banks and General Irwin McDowell in the valley.

On 22 March, Jackson sent cavalry to attack a detachment of Banks' army at Kernstown; the next day, he pitched in his infantry. Initially, the attack made progress, but then Banks counterattacked and sent the Rebels running. Jackson lost 700 of 4200 men engaged, the Union 590 of 9000. Apparently, it was close to a debacle, but ultimately, Jackson's defeat at Kernstown turned out to be as good as a major victory for the South.

In Washington, Lincoln and his cabinet were shaken by this Confederate show of strength in the Shenandoah and immediately threw over plans for Banks and McDowell to reinforce McClellan. In turn, McClellan became even more cautious and tentative than usual, with fatal consequences for his Peninsular Campaign toward Richmond. Thus Jackson's defeat at Kernstown may have prolonged the war by three years. The diversion was already working handsomely.

Washington ordered the separate commands of Banks, McDowell, and, to the west, General John C Frémont, to deal with Jackson. With Banks beginning a cautious pursuit and the other Federal forces advancing, Jackson withdrew south up the valley with his 6000 men, a strategy taking shape in his mind.

Above: *The Army of the Potomac makes a night march into Virginia across the river that gave them their name.*

Far left: *The Union's Pennsylvania Bucktails attack part of Stonewall Jackson's army in the Shenandoah Valley near Harrisonburg, Virginia – 28 June 1862. From a sketch by Edwin Forbes, war correspondent for* Leslie's Illustrated Newspaper.

Left: *John C Frémont had a checkered career as a surveyor, explorer, soldier, businessman, and Union general. Having been court-martialed in 1847 for mutiny against his superior during California's revolt against Mexico (which Frémont had actively instigated), the colorful Pathfinder, as he was called, promptly got President James Polk to remit his sentence of mutiny. When the Civil War broke out, he purchased arms for the Union at his own expense and was given command of the Department of the West and then of western Virginia, where he was defeated by Jackson in 1862.*

Jackson was a strange, secretive man, shabby in his dress, devoutly religious (he usually declined to fight on Sunday), and a wildcat on the battlefield. Robert E Lee would write of him, 'A man he is of contrasts so complete that he appears on one day a Presbyterian deacon . . . and, the next, a reincarnated Joshua. He lives by the New Testament and fights by the Old.' The heart of his concept of strategy, Jackson said, was, 'Always mystify, mislead, and surprise the enemy.' His Valley Campaign would be the perfect demonstration of that maxim – and one of the great military operations in history.

As Banks marched in pursuit, Jackson suddenly made a forced march to Swift Run Gap, in the eastern mountains, which placed him on Banks's flank and forced the Yankee general to stop and protect his supply line. Meanwhile, Jackson was re-inforced to a command of 17,000 men – his maximum strength.

His operation went into high gear when Jackson learned that Frémont's force was about to join Banks. That had to be prevented. Ordering some cavalry feints to hold Banks, Jackson took the rest of his men by train to Staunton, putting out the word that he was retreating (his own men believed so until they arrived at Staunton). Jackson was actually taking a roundabout route to the town of McDowell, whence he went from Staunton by forced march. So fast did the Southerners move – up to 30 miles a day – that they took to calling themselves the 'foot cavalry.'

At McDowell on 8 May, Jackson confronted some 6000 Federals who were on their way to join Frémont. The Yankees attacked Jackson's force of 10,000, but the Confederates struck back and chased the enemy into West Virginia. Jackson then headed his men for Harrisonburg. At that point, as far as the Federals were concerned, Jackson disappeared from the face of the earth. On 23 May, with his full contingent, he came apparently from nowhere to strike Union troops at Front Royal; his men captured or killed 904 of the 1063-man garrison.

Learning of the disaster at Front Royal, Banks pulled his men back from Strasburg to high ground at Winchester. Before he could dig in, however, Jackson was on him – after an all-night forced march. He attacked the Federals on both flanks and dealt the final blow in the center. Banks withdrew across the Potomac and was out of the valley for good; he had lost some 3000 men of 8000 in his command. Jackson's casualties were some 400 of 16,000. After resting for a couple of days, Jackson marched to Harpers Ferry, where he was soon threatened by the converging forces of Frémont and McDowell.

Jackson left the Stonewall Brigade to prevent Banks from recrossing the Potomac and pulled the rest of his men south on 30 May. When his forces were widely scattered, he learned that the two Union generals were coming on fast, so he sent detachments to hold them up, concentrated his forces, and continued south with 15,000 men and a double wagon train of captured supplies 7 miles long. His pursuers could make only weak strikes on Jackson's rear; he had burned all the bridges. But by 7 June McDowell and Frémont had caught Jackson squarely between them. The most remarkable achievement of the campaign ensued when Federal units began picking away at Jackson's flanks from the east and west. On 8 June, Frémont advanced from Cross Keys, but Richard Ewell's division of 6500 stopped Frémont's 10,500 in their tracks. With Frémont kept at bay by a burned bridge, Jackson struck the other Union detachment at Port Republic with his full force the next day. After heavy fighting, the Federals were driven back.

That was the end of an extraordinary campaign. With some 16,000 men, Jackson had bested 50,000 Union troops by outmaneuvering and outnumbering his enemy in nearly every engagement – he had, in military terms, 'defeated the enemy in detail.' In 1 month, his men had marched more than 250 miles, fought 4 pitched battles and constant skirmishes, and captured more than 400 prisoners and enormous quantities of arms and supplies. It had been a historic demonstration of mobile striking power (one that the Germans would study with profit before World War II). As Jackson marched his men east to rejoin Robert E Lee in Virginia, the war in the Eastern Theater was firmly under Confederate control.

Left: *The Confederate First Virginia Cavalry in the field, as sketched by A R Waud.*

Above: *Front Royal, Virginia, where Jackson's men made a surprise attack that nearly wiped out the Union garrison of more than 1000 men: Shenandoah Valley Campaign, 23 May 1862.*

Right: *A Confederate artilleryman of 1862 with ordnance – a siege artillery piece. The principal factor in choosing the size of siege guns was the difficulty of getting them to the scene of action by a team of horses. The 24-pounder smoothbore was of near-maximum weight – about five tons – and required a ten-horse team to shift it on a good surface.*

The Peninsular Campaign and the Seven Days' Battles

It was only after a great deal of prodding from Lincoln that General George B McClellan, in mid-March 1862, shipped the 112,000 troops of his new Army of the Potomac to Fort Monroe, Virginia, at the tip of the peninsula between the James and York Rivers. The goal of their Peninsular Campaign was the Confederate capital of Richmond. Because of the demands of the campaign, and McClellan's reluctance to respond to orders, Lincoln relieved the general from overall command of the Union armies and took on those duties himself, with unfortunate results. Although Lincoln often had sound strategic ideas, he lacked the means to implement them.

McClellan had been deprived of expected reinforcements when Jackson tied up McDowell and Banks in the Shenandoah, but the Army of the Potomac could still have marched virtually unimpeded into Richmond – at that point there were fewer than half as many troops in McClellan's way as in his command.

The trouble was that his head of intelligence, Alan Pinkerton, consistently overestimated enemy strength by a wide margin. Thus throughout his career in the war, McClellan would proceed under the assumption that he was outnumbered, when the opposite was invariably the case.

To his credit, McClellan knew perfectly well that Jackson's operations in the Shenandoah were a diversion. But in his increasingly strident and insubordinate letters to Washington, the Union commander was never able to convince Lincoln of that fact, or to get the reinforcements he demanded. He began inching the Army of the Potomac up the peninsula toward Richmond, then stopped before Southern defenses that stretched from Yorktown across the peninsula. After looking them over, he reported to Washington that these defenses were 'one of the most extensive known to modern times.' In fact, they were manned by only 15,000 Confederates under General John B

Left: *Yorktown, Virginia, occupied by the Union Army of the Potomac in March 1862, at the beginning of the Peninsular Campaign.*

Above: *Union General Nathaniel B Banks clashed with Jackson's forces at Winchester, Virginia, on 25 May 1862. The Northerners had to retreat.*

Top right: *A Confederate camp in the Virginia woodlands.*

Far right: *Robert E Lee was 55 years old when he was given his first true field command by Confederate president Jefferson Davis. Lee took over the Army of Northern Virginia after General J E Johnston was wounded at the Battle of Seven Pines, or Fair Oaks, May 1862.*

Magruder. Drawing upon his experience as an amateur actor, Magruder proceeded to put on a show for the Yankees, parading troops in circles to convince McClellan that the barricades were swarming with soldiers. McClellan was quite ready to believe it. Although he could have stormed the position in a day, the Union commander spent a month preparing his assault, which gave General J E Johnston plenty of time to move some 45,000 reinforcements into the area and to improve the defenses around Richmond.

By the time McClellan mounted his assault at Yorktown, most of the enemy had pulled back to the new defenses. McClellan then resumed his cautious advance up the peninsula. In Washington, Lincoln groaned wearily to his Cabinet that the general had a bad case of 'the slows.' At the end of May, the Army of the Potomac was astride the Chickahominy River west of Richmond. General Johnston learned that Keyes's X Corps was isolated south of the river and determined to destroy it. The result was the Battle of Fair Oaks (or Seven Pines).

Johnston planned the battle well, setting up screens and secondary attacks. But General James Longstreet took the wrong route for his main attack and got in the way of other units, delaying until after noon the action that was to have begun at dawn. The ensuing fighting, amid marshy and wooded terrain, was fierce but disorganized. The Union men were driven back, then rallied and held on until McClellan was able to send reinforcements. Next day Longstreet renewed the attack at dawn, but made no progress against determined Federal resistance.

Although the Battle of Fair Oaks ended in failure for the Confederates, it did have one important outcome for the South. In the first day's fighting, General Johnston was severely wounded. His replacement was General Robert E Lee, who reorganized the troops and renamed them as history would know them – the Army of Northern Virginia. Lee was a gentle, aristocratic man from an old and distinguished Virginia family.

Until they found out how aggressive and brilliant he was his men were inclined to call him 'Granny.' It would not be long, however, before every soldier on both sides considered Lee the most dangerous man on the field.

After the Battle of Fair Oaks, McClellan and the Army of the Potomac remained along the Chickahominy, most on the south bank, but General Fitz-John Porter's V Corps on the north bank. Again, McClellan had left a detachment unsupported. From their camps, the Northerners could see the steeples of Richmond, nine miles away.

On 12 June, Lee asked his flamboyant cavalry leader J E B 'Jeb' Stuart to scout the Yankees. Stuart did a good deal more: he and 1200 troopers rode completely around the Army of the Potomac, raiding as they went. He returned to inform Lee of Porter's vulnerable position; Lee immediately decided to try and drive Porter's corps into the James River. Jackson had just arrived from the Shenandoah to join the action. The series of clashes that followed are known as the Seven Days' Battles.

As Lee prepared to attack, McClellan was finally ready to begin moving toward Richmond. In the first battle of the Seven Days, at Oak Grove on 25 June, McClellan drove into some Confederate outposts. In the next day's Battle of Mechanicsville, Lee took the initiative, sending General Magruder to make a feint – more theatrics – with his 25,000 men against the 60,000 Federals on the south bank. With his main body, Lee hoped to overwhelm Porter on the north bank. But Lee's complex plan of attack foundered, due mainly to the slowness of the exhausted Jackson and his men. Porter repulsed the Southerners easily.

The following day, Lee tried an assault on a new Federal defensive position at Gaines's Mill. In heavy fighting, with Jackson again lethargic, the V Corps was driven back before the Union line firmed up and the fighting ended inconclusively. Despite the fact that his men had stood up to the Southerners through two days of fighting, McClellan decided at that point to abandon the attempt on the Confederate capital and to withdraw back to Harrison's Landing.

The day of 28 June saw minor skirmishes at Garnett's and Golding's farms, west of Richmond. By the following day, the Army of the Potomac was withdrawing in good order to the southeast. In the last three battles of the Seven Days – Savage's Station, White Oak Swamp, and Malvern Hill – Lee made an unsuccessful attempt to turn that withdrawal into a rout. At Malvern Hill, he unwisely ordered an assault onto high ground and Union artillery tore the Southern lines to pieces.

Due largely to Jackson's uncharacteristic slowness, Lee had not managed the Army of Northern Virginia decisively and had lost 20,000 casualties in the Seven Days' Battles, compared to McClellan's 16,000. Nonetheless, Lee had driven the enemy away from his capital, which was no small achievement. And in the future, he would never again be subject to accusations of indecisiveness. As for McClellan – with immensely superior forces he had come within sight of Richmond in his Peninsular Campaign, but had been thoroughly outmaneuvered from start to finish. The soldiers of the Army of the Potomac had fought valiantly; to win battles, however, they needed a fighting general.

Below: *The Battle of Fair Oaks, nine miles from Richmond, was a Union victory that might have toppled the Confederate capital, but General McClellan failed to follow up on it.*

Right: *Confederate General Joseph E Johnston recovered from his wound at Fair Oaks to fight on until the war's end.*

Bottom right: *A cavalry charge by the Union's 5th Regulars at Gaines's Mill, the third of the Seven Days' Battles.*

Following pages: *A panoramic view of the Battle of Fair Oaks, after which President Lincoln exhorted McClellan to 'hold all your ground.' But the Peninsular Campaign had already bogged down.*

The Second Battle of Bull Run

After three separate commands had failed to run Stonewall Jackson to earth in the Shenandoah, Washington decided to combine those units into one – the short-lived Army of Virginia. Its commander, General John Pope, transferred from the Army of the Mississippi, started off badly with a blustering address that began, 'Let us understand each other. I have come to you from the West, where we have always seen the backs of our enemies.' In Richmond, after the Seven Days' Battles, Lee was outraged by such ungentlemanly behavior in wartime: 'the miscreant Pope,' he proclaimed, must be 'suppressed.' In mid-July 1862, Pope began marching his 50,000 troops toward union with McClellan's 90,000-man Army of the Potomac. Lee, with 80,000 men, had to prevent that juncture.

By then, Lee had grouped his command into the unit that would lead the Army of Northern Virginia to victory time and again: Stonewall Jackson, his strong right arm; his other divi-

sion commanders, James Longstreet, A P Hill, and D H Hill; and his cavalry leader, the brilliant Jeb Stuart. To stop Pope's march, Lee dispatched the commands of Jackson and A P Hill.

Jackson planned to strike Pope's advance and then try to defeat the Federals one corps at a time. But when the forces collided on 9 August in the Battle of Cedar Mountain, the Federals drove off Jackson's men and only a last-minute counterattack by A P Hill saved the day. Then McClellan began to pull troops away from Richmond and send them by ship to reinforce Pope. Now that McClellan no longer threatened the capital, Lee could move Longstreet's forces to join Jackson and Hill.

The opposing armies took up positions on opposite sides of the Rappahannock River, where Lee learned that McClellan's reinforcements would reach Pope in approximately five days. The Confederates had to take care of Pope first. It was then that the team of Lee and Jackson took fire.

Above: *Two Union brigades drive Confederate forces from the woods at the Battle of Cedar Mountain, 9 August 1862.*

Left: *Union forces lost some 1700 men at Cedar Mountain, the first engagement of the Second Bull Run (Second Manassas) Campaign.*

Right: *Union General John Pope led 62,000 men into battle at Second Bull Run but was repulsed by a much smaller Confederate force led by Jackson and James Longstreet. After he was relieved of command, Pope blamed subordinates, including General Fitz-John Porter, for the loss at Bull Run.*

Following pages: *The Second Battle of Bull Run, fought on 29-30 August 1862, was the climax of a victorious Confederate campaign that saved Richmond and rid Virginia of enemy troops.*

At West Point it was drilled into future officers that they must never divide forces in the face of the enemy. For the first of several times Lee did just that, even though he knew that Pope's forces outnumbered his. Longstreet was ordered to spread his command along the Rappahannock and hold the Federals in place while Jackson was sent out on a wide envelopment. On 27 August, Jackson destroyed a Union supply dump at Manassas, in Pope's rear, and then disappeared.

A furious Pope put his army on the march, in a futile attempt to find and destroy Jackson. On 28 August the Federals were at Groveton; nearby, Jackson had concealed his men in a railroad cut. At that point Jackson faced a dilemma: he had only a third of Pope's strength and Lee and Longstreet were still some distance away, but if the Federals moved into strong defenses at Centreville, they could hold out until McClellan's reinforcements arrived. Taking a historic gamble, Jackson feinted at Pope, revealing his position.

Pope gleefully gave orders to smash Jackson, meanwhile ignoring intelligence reports that warned of Longstreet's approach. The Second Battle of Bull Run broke out on the morning of 29 August when Pope's 62,000 men made a series of unco-ordinated frontal assaults on Jackson's 20,000. Well protected in the railroad cut, the Confederates mowed down the oncoming Federals. (Only late in the war would it be realized that one man firing from cover was worth three men charging at him.)

The Union assaults continued through the morning, leaving row after row of dead in front of the railroad cut. The outcome became a question of time: would Jackson run out of ammunition before Longstreet arrived? Stonewall began riding along his lines, shouting to his exhausted troops, 'Two hours, men! In two hours you will have help. You must stand it two hours!' And then, 'Half an hour, men! Can you stand it half an hour?'

They stood it, and at 11 o'clock in the morning Longstreet arrived and mounted a probing attack in the Federal center, relieving the pressure on Jackson. Pope persisted in ignoring the presence of Longstreet and maintained that Jackson was retreating. Next day Pope learned better. After letting the Federals strike Jackson's left, Lee sent Longstreet into a crushing assault on the opposite Union flank, catching Pope in a pincers. The Federals had no choice but to run for their lives. The two days of fighting had claimed 1724 Union men killed, 8372 wounded; 1481 Southerners had died and 7627 were wounded.

The Second Battle of Bull Run (known to the South as Second Manassas) marked the completion of a long and ultimately victorious campaign that included Jackson's Shenandoah Valley operations and the Seven Days' Battles. When Lee took command, McClellan had been at the gates of Richmond; since then, Lee had defeated two superior Federal armies and virtually cleared Virginia of enemy forces. Now the Confederate leader was only 25 miles from Washington, the North's capital. He began to plan an invasion of the North with his triumphant Army of Northern Virginia.

Right: *Union General Franz Sigel's corps took part in the fight at Bull Run after Sigel had succeeded John Frémont in the newly created Army of Virginia. Frémont had resigned on account of his antipathy to General Pope.*

Below: *The railroad junction at Manassas made it the focal point of two major engagements, in 1861 and 1862. Here a Union officer leads a charge on the railroad embankment during the Second Battle of Bull Run.*

The Battle of Shiloh

By the middle of 1862, Lee and Jackson were dominating the Eastern theater of the war. In the Western theater, which included most of the Deep South, there were no comparable Confederate commanders of major armies. And in the first full year of fighting, the linked disciplines of strategy, tactics, and intelligence-gathering had not reached the high level they would later attain on both sides. A prime example of that fact was the Battle of Shiloh, which set the pattern of Union dominance in the Western theater.

In order to win the war, the North had to invade and occupy the South. Washington's first major task in that direction was to split the Confederacy from north to south by gaining control of the Mississippi River. Fresh from his victories at Forts Henry and Donelson, General Ulysses S Grant was preparing for new operations in the area in March 1962. The bulk of his Union Army of the Mississippi was encamped on the western bank of the Tennessee River near Pittsburg Landing, Tennessee, awaiting reinforcements from Don Carlos Buell's Army of the Ohio.

Meanwhile, in nearby Corinth, Mississippi, an important rail-road center, General Albert Sidney Johnston had assembled an army of 40,000 men for the purpose of destroying Grant. His second in command was General P G T Beauregard. Johnston's plan was to spring a surprise attack, envelop the Union left flank by the river (cutting off Buell's reinforcements), and then drive the Federals back against Owl Creek for the kill.

Before dawn on 6 April, Grant left Pittsburg Landing and his 33,000 troops (most of them inexperienced) to confer with General Buell in Savannah, Tennessee. Although Grant knew about the enemy concentration in Corinth, he had recently written to Henry Halleck, the new Union General in Chief, 'I scarcely have the faintest idea of an attack . . . being made on us.' Grant and his close subordinate William Tecumseh Sherman figured the Confederates would stay put in their strong defenses in Corinth.

They were disastrously wrong. Soon after Grant left on 6 April, Johnston's attack smashed into the camps of the sleeping

Right: *William T Sherman, who fought his way to prominence in the Union Army, was Grant's right hand in the Western theater battle of Shiloh, Tennessee: 6-7 April 1862,*

Below: *The Battle of Shiloh took more lives than any other engagement of the war to that date. More than 100,000 troops were involved, of whom almost 3500 were killed. An additional 16,400 were wounded.*

Federals, scattering many of them in panic. It appeared that a rout was imminent. But over on the left flank, where Johnston had planned his envelopment, one of Sherman's brigades stood their ground and fought back. The surprised Confederates pulled up, slowing the whole advance.

Thousands of raw Yankee recruits had a terrible baptism of fire that day, yet by midmorning scattered bands were beginning to resist the Confederate onslaught. Johnston allowed his attack to become disorganized – units intermingled, commands became confused, and the intended envelopment became a disorderly piecemeal advance. Meanwhile, Grant had arrived back at Pittsburg Landing and began to organize his resistance: General Lew Wallace was ordered to rush his 5000 troops from Crump's Landing, Buell was hurried, Union stragglers were rounded up at gunpoint. On the left center, a group of Federals under General Benjamin Prentiss fought back so fiercely that the Confederates dubbed the area the 'Hornet's Nest.' Grant ordered Prentiss to hold out as long as possible.

The initial Southern impetus was finally lost in midafternoon, when General A S Johnston, whom the Confederacy considered one of its greatest hopes, died after a stray bullet cut an artery in his leg. His replacement, General Beauregard, had opposed the whole offensive from the beginning – moreover, he was quite sick that day.

As the afternoon ended, Grant was still in desperate shape. His left had been driven back almost to Pittsburg Landing, where Buell's reinforcements had to come in. The Hornet's Nest was gradually overrun after 11 separate charges; Prentiss surrendered in late afternoon. But the effort it took to round up Prentiss's 2200 Federals wasted valuable time for the South. By the time the Confederates made their last push of the day, Union batteries and gunboats were in position to slow the advance. At the same time, Buell's reinforcements arrived on the opposite bank and began to be ferried over; not realizing that, Beauregard called off the fighting about six o'clock. The decision probably cost him the battle.

That night the Confederates slept in the captured Yankee camps, convinced that the next day would complete their victory. They could scarcely have known that U S Grant was not the surrendering type. All through a rainy and miserable night, Grant was busy organizing his forces – which now included 25,000 reinforcements from Buell – for a counterattack.

Early on the morning of 7 April, Grant unleashed his attack; by early afternoon his men had recaptured their camps. For a time the Southerners mounted fierce resistance near Beauregard's headquarters at Shiloh Church, which would give the battle its name. But the Confederate commander had only 20,000 men left fighting, and reinforcements from the west had been halted by high water on the Mississippi. At 2:30 PM Beauregard gave the order to retreat to Corinth.

The Battle of Shiloh was the bloodiest of the war to date: 1754 Federals were killed and 8408 wounded of 62,682 engaged; the South had lost 1723 killed, 8012 wounded, of 40,335 engaged. None of the commanders had managed his troops well, although Grant had mounted a brilliant counterattack after being surprised on the first day. On the whole, it had been a 'soldier's battle,' a matter of the courage and resourcefulness of individual units. And the Union victory was incomplete since Southern forces had escaped to Corinth. Still, the Confederacy would never be as strong again in Tennessee, and the North was one step closer to conquering the Mississippi.

His loss damaged Beauregard's reputation for the rest of the war. In Washington, some called for Grant's head, since he had been surprised at the outset and had failed to pursue the enemy to Corinth. To those demands Lincoln responded (thinking no doubt of McClellan's timidity), 'I can't spare this man. He fights.'

Right: *Confederate fortunes in the Western theater would suffer heavily from the loss of the gifted General Albert Sidney Johnston at Shiloh.*

Below: *The Tennessee River town of Pittsburg Landing was the scene of the Battle of Shiloh, which took its name from a church on the battlefield. The Union victory here helped set the stage for the conquest of the Mississippi.*

Left: *Ulysses S Grant receives his commission as lieutenant-general from President Lincoln.*

Following pages: *The 14th Regiment of Wisconsin Volunteers charge a New Orleans battery on the second day of the Battle of Shiloh.*

The Battle of Antietam

After his spectacular defeat of General Pope in the Second Battle of Bull Run, Robert E Lee decided to follow up his victory by invading the North through Maryland. With that fateful decision, he turned from a strategy of defending Confederate territory to one of conquest. Among other things, he hoped the operation would end fighting in his beloved Virginia, threaten Washington, and help the Confederacy gain recognition from European countries and thereby open up markets for the faltering Southern economy. All these were reasonable goals, but in the end, the invasion of Maryland would accomplish none of them.

On 7 September 1862, the Army of Northern Virginia began crossing the Potomac toward a concentration in Frederick, Maryland. On the Northern side, General McClellan was back in grace after the humiliation of General Pope. McClellan put the Army of the Potomac on the march to shadow Lee – slowly, as always. Knowing the indecisiveness of his opponent, Lee once again boldly split his forces; via Special Order Number 191, he sent a detachment under Jackson to capture Harpers Ferry, Virginia, to protect the entrance to the Shenandoah Valley. With Longstreet's command, Lee then continued north to Hagerstown. Soon after, a Federal soldier resting in a field picked up from the grass an envelope containing two cigars wrapped in a piece of paper. That paper was a copy of Lee's Special Order

Number 191, giving the exact disposition of all his forces. By nightfall, McClellan had the order and was crowing, 'Here is a paper with which, if I cannot whip Bobby Lee, I will be willing to go home!' It was never determined who had lost the order, but that same night Lee learned from Jeb Stuart that McClellan had it and began desperately to pull his forces together.

All McClellan needed to smash Lee one detachment at a time was a little speed. He moved the Army of the Potomac west with, for him, unusual dispatch. But it was not quite fast enough. The Army of the Potomac, some 110,000 strong, arrived on the east bank of Antietam Creek, near Sharpsburg, on 15 September. Across the creek was General Lee with only 19,000 men, awaiting the arrival of Jackson's 40,000 from Harpers Ferry. Even if Jackson made it in time, Lee would have to fight an enemy nearly twice his size with the Potomac at his back. Had McClellan attacked on the morning of 16 September, he would have rolled right over Lee and perhaps ended the war. Instead, the Union general let the opportunity of the lost orders slip through his fingers: as McClellan spent the 16th arranging his forces, Jackson arrived and Lee decided to stand and fight. This audacious decision was a testimony to the Confederate commander's low opinion of McClellan, and, as always, Lee knew his man.

What plan of battle McClellan made is not known; at least, none of his corps commanders seem to have been aware of it. By happenstance, then, the gigantic and terrible Battle of Antietam unfolded in three stages on 17 September. The first stage began when General Joseph Hooker took his I Corps out across a cornfield to attack the Union right flank. His goal was a little white Dunker church on high ground beyond the cornfield. Behind the church was the center of the Confederate line; if Hooker could take that position, he would fatally divide Lee's army.

Few of Hooker's men made it through the cornfield. A storm of fire erupted from Confederate batteries and flanking fire poured in from the West Woods. The Federals pressed on despite hundreds of casualties, then found themselves fighting hand-to-hand with Rebels in the tall corn. Finally, a tangled mass of Yankees emerged from the field and headed for the church; there they were met by a furious counterattack from John B Hood's Texas Brigade. After taking a volley that mowed down their line like a scythe, the Federals turned and ran. By that time Hooker was wounded and off the field, and his I Corps had suffered 2500 casualties. Southern losses in that area approached 50 percent. A drive into the cornfield by Joseph Mansfield's XII Corps did little but add to the dead, among them General Mansfield. However, G S Greene's brigade made it past the church and briefly pushed right through the frayed Southern line.

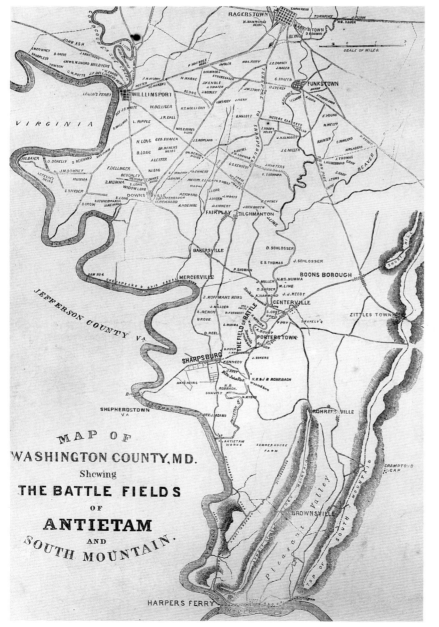

Left: A map of the Civil War era shows the battlefield at Sharpsburg, Maryland, Antietam Creek, and environs. Lee's ill-fated invasion of Maryland in a drive on the North would achieve none of the objectives that he had sought.

Top right: The First Maryland Battery appears in the foreground of this sketch made by A R Waud at the Battle of Antietam.

Right: A nearby house and barns burn down during the fighting at Antietam, in another sketch by A R Waud.

Above: *Union advance against the Confederate center behind the Dunker church.*

Left: *Artillerymen fire their weapons.*

Right: *The Northern victory at Antietam was the signal for Lincoln's Emancipation Proclamation of 22 September 1862. Instead of gaining the foreign recognition and support it had hoped to realize through the invasion of Maryland, the Confederacy had precipitated a political coup that made it impossible for any European power to take up the Southern cause.*

The second phase of the battle then developed in the center, where the II Corps under Edwin V Sumner moved to the attack. Expecting that, Lee had steadily been stripping his other positions to shore up the middle. Before he could stop it, though, General Sedgwick's division of the II Corps emerged from the West Wood right into a gap in the Southern line. For a few moments all was silent, as Sedgwick arranged his forces for the final blow. Then the reinforcements arrived with a hail of shot and shell that hit the Federals on three sides. Within 15 minutes, Sedgwick's division was fleeing back to their lines, leaving 2500 casualties behind – half their number. The pursuing Confederates also drove Greene back from the church.

The struggle in the middle ended after a heroic Union drive to claim a Rebel position in a sunken road, which would be remembered as Bloody Lane for the ghastly fighting that took place there. Spearheaded by the Irish Brigade, the Federals claimed the lane filled with Confederate dead, and from there mounted assaults that the Southerners were barely able to turn back. As Lee's army tottered again on the verge of ruin, McClellan ordered the rest of Sumner's II Corps to support the attack. Upon receiving Sumner's reply that he had no functional forces left, McClellan might have committed 25,000 fresh troops that he had in reserve. Instead, he ordered a pullback in the center and looked for progress on the left flank, where the third phase of the battle began.

There General Ambrose E Burnside had spent the day losing dozens of troops in trying to cross a bridge over the Antietam whose every inch was covered by enemy guns. (In a forecast of ineptitudes to come, Burnside had failed to discover that he could have waded his men across the creek at almost any point.) Finally, in early afternoon, the bridge was secured; after two hours' delay, Burnside sent his men marching toward Sharpsburg, driving the weakened Confederates before them. Then, as final victory was in sight for the Union, A P Hill's force arrived on the run from Harpers Ferry and shot the Federal advance to pieces. Both sides fell exhausted into their positions, and the great battle was over. Hill's arrival had kept the Confederacy alive.

Casualties at Antietam (or Sharpsburg) were the worst of any single day in the war. Of 75,316 Union effectives, there were 2108 dead, 9549 wounded, 753 missing – a total of 12,410 casualties. The South lost 2700 dead, 9024 wounded, 2000 missing of 51,844 effectives. On the battlefield, Antietam was clearly a stalemate, and a brilliant stand by Lee against vastly superior forces. It was only the aftermath that made it a Union victory.

Lee pulled back to Virginia on 18 September, his invasion of the North stymied. Just as importantly, President Lincoln had been waiting for a victory (or at least the appearance of one) to release one of the epochal documents in American history: the Emancipation Proclamation. Even though the document declared that only slaves within the Confederacy were free, and therefore actually freed none at all, it was still the beginning of the end of human slavery in the United States. By transforming the war from a struggle against secession to one against slavery, the proclamation made it impossible for any European country to recognize and trade freely with the Confederacy; now the South would have to depend on its own steadily declining resources. The Emancipation Proclamation was not only a landmark in freeing America from a longstanding evil, it was also one of Lincoln's political masterstrokes.

Right: *President Lincoln visits the battlefield at Antietam in a photograph published in Gardner's Sketch Book of the Civil War – October 1862.*

Bottom left: *Bloody Lane, filled with the bodies of Confederate artillerymen.*

Below: *A lithograph of 1863 depicting Lincoln writing the Emancipation Proclamation.*

Debacle at Fredericksburg

For public consumption, Lincoln had proclaimed Antietam a great victory for General McClellan and the Union. Privately, he knew better. In October, after Jeb Stuart had led his cavalrymen on a second humiliating ride around the Army of the Potomac, McClellan set out after Lee at his usual inchworm pace. Lincoln had had enough of the Little Napoleon; he cashiered McClellan in November. But the general whom Lincoln named to head the Army of the Potomac was a choice born of desperation and miscalculation: Ambrose E Burnside, one of the most inept officers of that or any war.

Somehow, Burnside's blundering engagement at the bridge during Antietam had been interpreted as a great success, and the genial and handsome general was popular with both soldiers and the public. (His glorious whiskers gave the word 'sideburns' to the language). Burnside's strategy was simply to make a beeline for Richmond, en route occupying Fredericksburg, Virginia, which lay along the Rappahannock River. A Federal division arrived across the river from the town on 17 November, a day before Longstreet's command pulled in opposite. At that point, Burnside could easily have sent his men across the river and taken Fredericksburg. Instead, he collected his forces and waited more than three weeks to mount an attack. During that time, Lee arrived with the full Army of Northern Virginia and erected virtually impregnable defenses

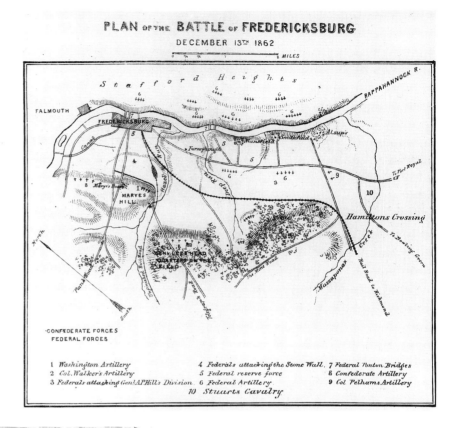

PLAN of the BATTLE of FREDERICKSBURG
DECEMBER 13TH 1862

·CONFEDERATE FORCES
  FEDERAL FORCES

1 Washington Artillery
2 Col. Walker's Artillery
3 Federals attacking Gen! A P Hill's Division.
4 Federals attacking the Stone Wall.
5 Federal reserve force
6 Federal Artillery
7 Federal Ponton Bridges
8 Confederate Artillery
9 Col. Pelham's Artillery
10 Stuarts Cavalry

Above: *Map showing the disposition of Union and Confederate forces at the Battle of Fredericksburg, Virginia, 13 December 1862.*

Left: *Pontoon bridge wagons on their way from Aquia Creek to the Rappahannock River for the Union assault on Fredericksburg.*

Right: *Union general Ambrose E Burnside, who lost 12,700 men in the bungled attack on strongly fortified Southern positions at Fredericksburg.*

behind the town. Although he had 78,500 men to Burnside's 122,000, Lee awaited the coming Federal attack with visible delight.

Finally, on 11 December, Federal troops began constructing pontoon bridges across the Rappahannock. Lee had no intention of stopping the crossing, but he had posted sharpshooters in the town who claimed dozens of Union casualties during the preparations. When the bridges were finished, the Army of the Potomac poured across the river and spent the night of the 12th in bivouac in the town. Many men and officers had a good idea of what horror they were in for the next day.

On the morning of 13 December, the area was blanketed by a thick fog. Suddenly, at ten o'clock, it swept away and revealed to the Southerners rank upon rank of Federals, their banners flying, preparing to attack. On the right, General William Franklin's division advanced on Stonewall Jackson's position; Jackson's artillery opened up, tearing wide holes in the Union lines until Jackson ordered a halt, deliberately letting the Yankees close in. When they were within rifle range, Jackson unleashed a terrific fire that stopped the advance in its tracks; he then mounted a counterattack that chased the Federals back down the hill. After three hours of terrible fighting, Franklin's division gave up.

The story was the same all down the line, all afternoon: wave after wave of Federals threw themselves toward the Southern positions, some units losing 50 percent and more in casualties. Entering the storm of lead and shells, the men bent forward, averting their faces, as if walking into a rainstorm. Longstreet would write of what he saw at the foot of Marye's Heights: 'At each attack the slaughter was so great that by the time the third attack was repulsed, the ground was so thickly strewn with dead that the bodies seriously impeded the approach of the Federals.' By the end of the day, when the battle subsided, not one Federal soldier had reached the Southern lines. Said a Northern participant, 'They might as well have tried to take Hell.'

Never in the war were so many lives and bodies, and so much heroism, squandered in a more tragic and stupid assault. At Fredericksburg the North lost 12,700 killed and wounded of 106,000 engaged; Lee's army lost less than half that – 5300 casualties of 72,500 engaged. That night, a survivor lying on the battlefield lay listening to the wounded, 'a wail so far and deep and wide, as if a thousand discords were flowing together into a key-note weird, unearthly, terrible to hear and bear.'

Burnside made one more attempt, ordering the Army of the Potomac to march upstream and attack Lee from behind. Coming as it did in the middle of a January thaw, the operation ground to a halt in a sea of mud. With that Mud March, as it was dubbed, Burnside had crowned a debacle with a fiasco. He was relieved at his own request at the end of January 1863.

Perhaps the best epitaph for the Union dead at Fredericksburg was written by their enemy, General Longstreet: 'The spectacle that we saw upon the battlefield was one of the most distressing I ever witnessed. The charges had been desperate and bloody, but utterly hopeless. I thought, as I saw the Federals come again and again to their death, that they deserved success if courage and daring could entitle soldiers to victory.'

Left: *Had the Union attack on Fredericksburg succeeded, nearby Richmond would have been the prize. But the Confederate capital remained safe for the time being.*

Above: *Wounded soldiers on Marye's Heights.*

Right: *Representatives of the Bureau of Military Railroads survey the wreckage of Confederate caisson wagons and their teams above Fredericksburg.*

Following pages: *The siege of Vicksburg, Mississippi.*

PART 3
The Decisive Year

The Battle of Stones River

It was during the course of 1863 that the impetus toward victory turned from the Confederacy to the Union once and for all. That year of decision began, however, with the indecisive Battle of Stones River near Murfreesboro, Tennessee. The two principal forces in western Tennessee at that time were the Federal Army of the Cumberland, under William S Rosecrans, and the Confederate Army of Tennessee under Braxton Bragg. Rosecrans was an effective organizer and administrator, but undependable in action. Bragg, who had just been thwarted in an attempted invasion of Kentucky, was an experienced officer and a favorite of Jefferson Davis; unfortunately for the South, however, Bragg was also argumentative, inflexible, disliked by his officers, and served badly by them.

On 31 December 1862, the two armies were poised for battle just west of Stones River. As happened more than once in the war, both commanders made the same plan – to attack the opposite right flank, which would have swung the armies in a circle if followed through. But battles seldom go as planned: at dawn Bragg's attack broke out first against the Federal right wing; heavy fighting surged back and forth for hours before the Union line was pushed back on the pivot of the left flank like a door. From that point, the Federals fought desperately to hold their line during several waves of attacks from Bragg.

The first day of the new year saw only minor skirmishing while both sides recouped. On 2 January, Bragg ordered General John C Breckinridge to assault a Federal position on a hill to the north; Breckinridge drove the defenders from the top of the hill, but as they pursued the retreat his men were mowed down by Federal artillery. Breckinridge was forced to withdraw with heavy losses, and the battle ended.

Nominally, Stones River was a tactical victory for the South, but Rosecrans's army was still intact and in practice the battle amounted to a bloody draw. The Union had lost 12,906 casualties of 41,400 engaged, the South 11,739 of 34,739 engaged. The results had less to do with good generalship than with the fighting spirit of the Confederates and the defensive resolution of the Union soldiers. The same would apply when the two armies met again at Chickamauga.

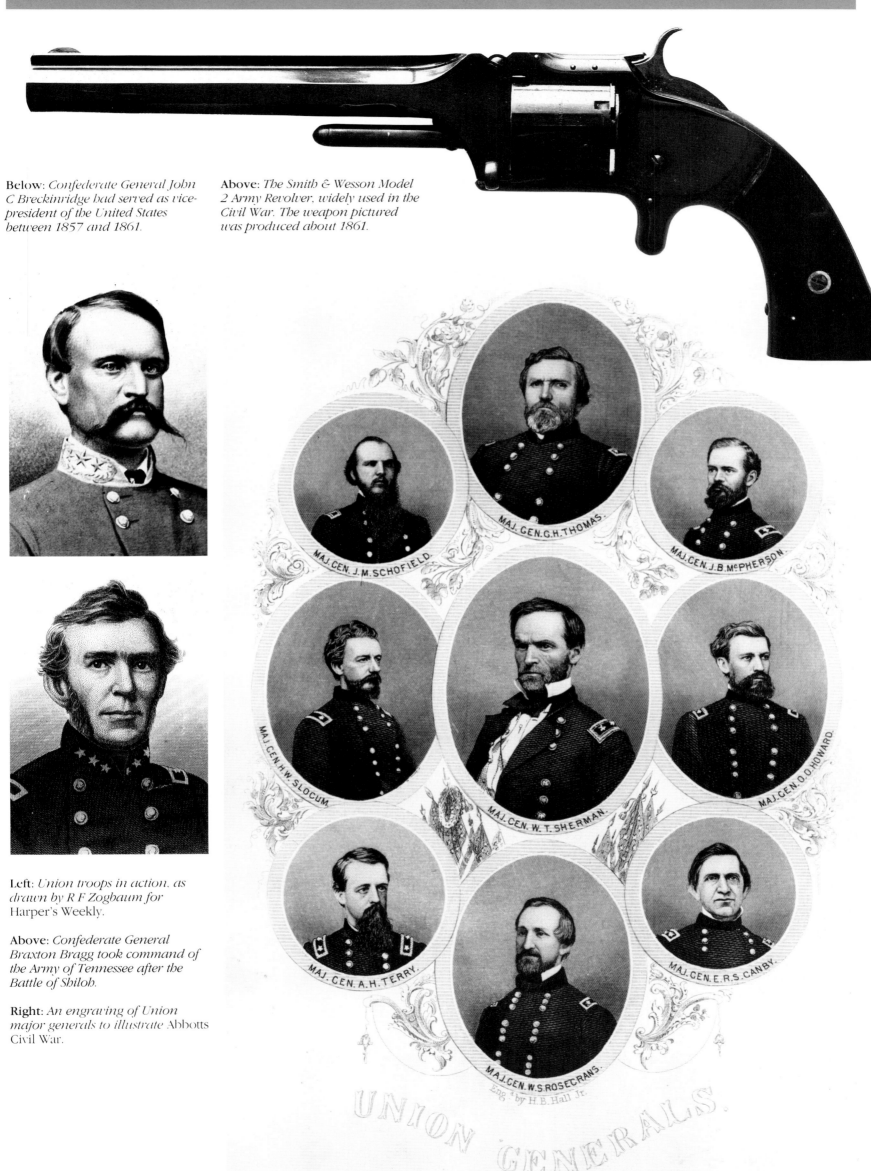

Below: *Confederate General John C Breckinridge had served as vice-president of the United States between 1857 and 1861.*

Above: *The Smith & Wesson Model 2 Army Revolver, widely used in the Civil War. The weapon pictured was produced about 1861.*

Left: *Union troops in action, as drawn by R F Zogbaum for* Harper's Weekly.

Above: *Confederate General Braxton Bragg took command of the Army of Tennessee after the Battle of Shiloh.*

Right: *An engraving of Union major generals to illustrate* Abbotts Civil War.

MAJ. GEN. J.M. SCHOFIELD.

MAJ. GEN. G.H. THOMAS.

MAJ. GEN. J.B. McPHERSON.

MAJ. GEN. H.W. SLOCUM.

MAJ. GEN. W.T. SHERMAN.

MAJ. GEN. O.O. HOWARD.

MAJ. GEN. A.H. TERRY.

MAJ. GEN. W.S. ROSECRANS.

MAJ. GEN. E.R.S. CANBY.

Eng^d by H.E. Hall Jr.

UNION GENERALS.

Left: *Union Admiral David Glasgow Farragut, who captured New Orleans in April 1862.*

Right: *A seaman of the Confederate Navy.*

Below: *The capture of Port Royal, South Carolina, by the Union fleet under Flag Officer S F du Pont gave the North a strategic position between Savannah and Charleston.*

the road, and aimed the captured gun down the track. The train derailed at top speed and the Federal guard was sent running by a round of grapeshot from the howitzer. Even though the guard pulled together and drove off the Irregulars, the Yankees suffered twelve casualties to Mosby's one.

After the war ended and the Irregulars went home unconquered, a Union general called Mosby's operations 'the only perfect success in the Southern Army.' The later career of the Gray Ghost was unique among former Southern officers: he became a friend and political supporter of Ulysses S Grant, who had ordered Mosby hanged if captured during the war. Mosby spent the last years of his life serving the government he had once fought so brilliantly.

Far left: *Mosby's Irregulars rendezvous by night in Virginia's Blue Ridge Mountains.*

Left: *Sketch of a Union cavalryman.*

Below: *A Union railroad battery built to defend workmen rebuilding bridges burned by Confederate raiders. The railroads were vital to both sides for transport of troops and supplies.*

Jeb Stuart Rides

The Civil War saw the last flowering of an ancient military elite – the horse cavalry. And the man who best exemplified that tradition was James Ewell Brown 'Jeb' Stuart, Lee's flamboyant commander of cavalry. Stuart considered himself a modern incarnation of a medieval knight and was pleased to be called 'The Cavalier.' With his cinnamon spade beard, ostrich-plumed hat, and tasselled uniform, he rather resembled a later Hollywood version of the Confederate cavalryman. Characteristic also were his doggerel poems in praise of his own exploits. There was something unreal about Jeb Stuart's style that reflected the South's fantasy of itself as a land of knights and chivalry, but his courage and his prowess were entirely real.

In his role as Lee's scout, Stuart's primary job was to be the eyes of the Army of Northern Virginia (Lee once said admiringly, 'He never brought me an incorrect piece of information'). His particular specialty was the strategic raid – striking behind enemy lines at communications, supply bases, factories, and railroads. The two rides around McClellan's Army of the Potomac were examples; although they looked something like a stunt, they accomplished considerable destruction and were undoubtedly a humiliation for the Union. Stuart's last ride around the Yankees, before Gettysburg, would be far less fruitful in its results.

Typical of the Cavalier's exploits was the 'Dumfries Raid' of late December 1862, one of a series of Stuart operations on Union communications that followed the Battle of Fredericksburg. With 1800 riders, Stuart crossed the Rappahannock River on Christmas Day and was soon driving Yankee cavalry from their camps near the town of Occoquan; in the process he bagged 100 prisoners and quantities of supplies, burning every-

thing he couldn't carry. He then took over a Federal telegraph station and listened in on messages detailing efforts to capture him; Stuart replied by wiring Washington to complain about the quality of the Yankee mules he'd captured. By the end of the year, he and his men had returned from their raids with 200 prisoners, 200 horses, 20 Federal wagons, and a fine haul of supplies and weapons.

There were equally brilliant raiding and scouting operations for some time after that. Before the battle of Chancellorsville, for example, Stuart made the Confederate victory possible by detecting an unprotected Union flank. In the long run, though, he suffered from the trouble common to successful tacticians: one's enemies tend to learn from their tactics and turn them against their originators. Eventually, the Federal cavalry, particularly a bantamweight fighter named Philip Sheridan, would learn their lessons from Stuart and then dispose of their teacher.

Below: *Stuart's cavalrymen intercept the 5th US Cavalry near Tunstall's Station, Virginia, in the summer of 1862.*

Right: *Stuart sat for his portrait in full regalia, including his famous plumed hat and the curved saber of the cavalryman.*

Above: *A war correspondent's sketch of the cavalry action near Boonesborough during the invasion of Maryland.*

Left: *A romantic turn-of-the-century painting of Stuart's first ride around the Army of the Potomac.*

Right: *Stuart's 10-day absence on a scouting mission had grim results for Lee's army, marching blind into enemy territory around Gettysburg, Pennsylvania.*

The Wartime South

The South clearly possessed superior military leadership at the beginning of the war, but on the political front it lacked anything approaching a Lincoln, his Cabinet, or an effectual Congress. Confederate President Jefferson Davis had much experience in both government and the military – a graduate of West Point, he had been a soldier, a senator, and Secretary of War under Franklin Pierce. As a politician, however, Davis was cold, uncompromising, and dictatorial. He controlled the overall military strategy of the Confederacy, often to its detriment: among other failings, he had a tendency to favor bad generals (like Bragg) and hamstring good ones (like Nathan Bedford Forrest). The South needed either a first-rate politician or a first-rate military leader as president: Davis was neither. Adding to the difficulty was an unco-operative and inefficient Confederate Congress, whose members resented Davis's autocracy and fought regularly among themselves as well. Finally, Vice-President Alexander H Stephens was bitterly opposed to many of Davis's policies and resisted the president at every turn.

A primary result of these problems at the top was that the Southern economy deteriorated steadily during the war. Inflation was so bad that in Charleston, South Carolina, in early 1863, a loaf of bread cost $25 in Confederate money. That spring, bread riots broke out in Richmond; Davis appeared in person to disperse the mob. Although the Confederate government was able to supply its troops adequately with arms and war materiel, it was dismally ineffective in providing food and clothing – Southern troops often marched and fought ragged, hungry, and shoeless. These political failures had a debilitating effect on the Southern war effort, especially in view of the South's disadvantages in men and money.

Above: *Confederate Secretary of the Treasury Charles G Memminger was up against the fact that the North had four-fifths of the nation's bank deposits when the war broke out and an even greater lead in manufacturing facilities (85 percent). These financial deficits were worsened by the Union blockade of Southern ports, which resulted in dwindling revenues for the Confederacy throughout the war years.*

Left: *The burning of Baton Rouge, the capital of Louisiana.*

Right: *Judah P Benjamin served the Confederacy as Attorney General, Secretary of War, and Secretary of State.*

Chancellorsville: Lee's Masterpiece

At the end of January 1863, command of the Army of the Potomac passed from the hapless Burnside to General Joseph Hooker. 'Fighting Joe' was one of the few Federal officers who genuinely wanted the job of trying to bring down Robert E Lee; he had schemed for months to get it. A strikingly handsome old army man, Hooker had the usual officer's vices, only more so: his fondness for the bottle and the ladies was legendary (although the notion that the popular term for prostitutes came from his name is a myth).

In taking command, Hooker issued the inevitable lion-hearted manifesto: 'May God have mercy on General Lee, for I will have none!' He meticulously rebuilt the twice-defeated, once-tied Army of the Potomac, meanwhile evolving his plan of attack: leaving a detachment to keep the Confederates in their present position at Fredericksburg, he would march his major forces around in a wide envelopment to come in behind the unsuspecting Lee from the west. It was a good plan and might have worked very well, if Lee had been willing to follow it.

Hooker had paid particular attention to building up his cavalry; in mid-April he dispatched all 12,000 horsemen under General George Stoneman to tear up the Confederate supply lines. Stoneman was no Jeb Stuart and his raid proved ineffectual; at the outset the troopers were held up for nearly two weeks by floods and thereafter they ranged around to little purpose. Lee and Stuart simply ignored the Yankee cavalry.

On 27 April 1863, Hooker put his plan into motion, pulling 80,000 troops out of their camps across the river from Fredericksburg and leaving 40,000 under General Sedgwick to hold the Army of Northern Virginia in place. For weeks, Lee had been expecting some such move. Soon Jeb Stuart reported that the main body of Federals was gathering at a little road crossing and clearing called Chancellorsville and preparing to march on the Southern rear.

Lee had sent two divisions out to forage and had on hand 60,000 men – only about half Hooker's strength. Once again, Lee reached into his mental file of enemy officers, took stock of General Hooker, and decided to fight. As he had done at the Second Bull Run and Antietam, he violated the old military rule and split his forces on the verge of battle, sending most of his men toward Chancellorsville and leaving a screening force of only 10,000 at Fredericksburg. The latter were ordered to build a lot of fires that night to fool the Yankees.

Part of Hooker's strategy had been to push past the thick woods – called the Wilderness – that surrounded Chancellorsville. If he could fight Lee on open ground, superior Union artillery would have clear lines of fire and the army could readily maneuver. On 1 May, the Army of the Potomac was marching out of the Wilderness as planned, and gathering on high ground some two miles from the small crossroads town in the woods. Then, at midmorning, skirmishers on the Federal

Below left: *Stonewall Jackson was devoutly religious and frequently led his men in prayer.*

Right: *The loss to the Confederacy in Jackson's death at Chancellorsville was incalculable. He was not only Lee's ablest commander, but one of the pre-eminent figures of American military history. By early 1863, the superiority in leadership that the South had enjoyed earlier in the war was eroding rapidly.*

Following pages: *A Confederate camp near Chancellorsville, Virginia, in 1863. The South had the advantage of fighting most of the war on its own ground with civilian aid and support.*

advance suddenly ran into a line of Confederates. For a while the enemies simply stood there blinking at one another.

The Federal commanders began to pull their units up into line of battle. For some hours, however, Hooker was strangely inactive. Then he issued an order that astonished and enraged his generals: they were to pull back into the Wilderness and set up defensive positions. At the first brush with Robert E Lee, Joe Hooker had precipitously abandoned his grand battle plan. One infantryman recalled of the pullback, 'The soldiers were as discomfited as if they had been checked by a serious repulse . . . Before the discharge of a single gun . . . somebody had again blundered.'

As the Army of the Potomac entrenched in the Wilderness that afternoon, Jeb Stuart roamed around the Yankees, probing for a weak spot. In the afternoon he found it: the XI Corps, posi-

tioned on the Union right, was unprotected on the flank – 'in the air,' as it was called. Within the Confederate lines that night, Lee and Stonewall Jackson sat on cracker boxes warming their hands over a fire and talking in quiet voices. They were planning another unpleasant surprise for Joe Hooker.

On 2 May, the Federals waited as morning passed into noon. Hooker began to speculate that Lee was retreating. Vague reports kept coming in of some sort of enemy movement across his front; General Daniel E Sickles took his men into the woods and captured a few of Jackson's men, one of whom jeered, 'You wait until Jackson gets around on your right!' Hooker dismissed these taunts. In midafternoon the soldiers of the XI Corps began to sense that something was gathering on their flank and sent word asking for support. Hooker ridiculed the requests.

Splendid Advance of Sykes's Regulars.

Centre of our Line of Battle

Around six o'clock in the afternoon, something very odd happened: a wave of rabbits and deer suddenly dashed into the positions of the XI Corps. The nervous soldiers whooped and laughed as the animals scampered to the rear. Then all laughing ceased, as the spine-chilling screech of the Rebel yell erupted from thousands of throats. From the woods at a dead run, 26,000 of Stonewall Jackson's men struck the XI Corps and swept them up like a gigantic broom. Jackson had marched 16 miles across the Federals' front to mount a devastating attack on the unguarded flank.

The first Hooker heard of the rout was when a rabble of terrified survivors began pouring into the clearing at Chancellorsville, where Union headquarters had been set up in a columned mansion. Hooker leaped onto his horse and rode through the fugitives, finding an artillery unit to shell the Confederate advance. General Alfred Pleasonton ordered some Pennsylvania cavalrymen into the enemy line to buy time. Knowing it was suicide, the troopers rode right into the middle of the oncoming soldiers and rattled them long enough for a Federal battery to turn and open up. Few of the Union riders came back. Finally, dozens of cannon were pouring shot and shell into the Confederates; that and the coming of night brought their advance to a halt. Both sides slept exhausted on the field. Then, at nine o'clock that night, disaster struck the Confederacy.

Stonewall Jackson had ridden out to reconnoiter in the dark, hoping to find a way of cutting off the Yankees if they tried a retreat. He roused some Northerners, who opened fire as Jackson and the others galloped back for their own lines. Hearing guns and approaching horsemen – and remembering the

Union cavalry charge of a few hours before – Confederates on both sides of the road started shooting into the dark; three bullets from his own men found Jackson. He was taken out in an ambulance, and his left arm had to be amputated. He began to succumb.

Elsewhere that night, fires started by the day's fighting raged in the Wilderness. Soldiers of both sides sat listening to screams within the flames: hundreds of wounded men were burning to death. Slowly, the cries grew fainter and ended. It was the kind of thing a soldier tries not to think about.

The next morning, with Jeb Stuart leading Jackson's command, the Confederates renewed the attack. Hooker seemed confused and despondent as shells began to burst around his headquarters at Chancellorsville. His army was being pushed back toward the Rappahannock. It was a different story miles away, at Fredericksburg: Hooker had ordered General Sedgwick to push past the enemy positions there and come in to hit

Lee from behind. In the morning, Sedgwick's men stormed the heights beneath which Burnside had squandered his army and headed for Chancellorsville. As Hooker waited on the porch of the mansion for Sedgwick's arrival, a cannonball splintered a column and the concussion knocked him to the ground. Dazed, he ordered a withdrawal to trenches already prepared between the Rapidan and the Rappahannock. With the Confederates swarming around them, the men of the Army of the Potomac retreated again.

Over in the Southern lines, a messenger galloped in to tell Lee of Sedgwick's approach. Lee smiled and told the messenger to rest, while he put the final touch on his masterpiece: leaving Stuart with 25,000 men to hold Hooker's retreating 75,000, Lee sent 20,000 troops to meet the new Federal contingent. Next morning, Sedgwick found himself surrounded on three sides and fled back to the Rappahannock.

With aggressiveness typical of him, Lee planned to assault the Federal entrenchments on 6 May. That might have gone very badly for the South because the positions were strong and the Yankees many. But the Northern general did not give Lee the chance; he withdrew across the Rappahannock on the night of 5 May. Hooker had gone into battle with twice the strength of his enemy and had let himself be outnumbered in every part of the engagement. Of 133,868 men, the Army of the Potomac had lost 17,278, to Lee's 12,821 casualties of 60,892 on the field. Years later, the Union general would confess of his inaction during the battle, 'To tell the truth, I just lost confidence in Joe Hooker.'

Chancellorsville had been Lee and Jackson's greatest victory, and it would be their last. On 10 May, the wounded Jackson cried out in delirium from his bed, 'Order A P Hill to prepare for action – pass the infantry to the front rapidly – tell Major Hawks . . . ' Then, after a silence, his last, strange words of peace: 'No, let us cross over the river and rest under the shade of the trees.'

Above: *Lee's bold attack on General Joseph Hooker's superior forces at Chancellorsville cut the Northern army in two, but Union troops were able to set up a defensive line – 2 May 1863, the day on which Stonewall Jackson received his fatal wound. That night Lee wrote to Jackson's chaplain, 'He has lost his left arm, but I have lost my right.' Jackson died of pneumonia and the effects of the amputation eight days later.*

Left: *General 'Fighting Joe' Hooker, who replaced Ambrose Burnside as commander of the Army of the Potomac.*

Right: *The last meeting of Robert E Lee and Stonewall Jackson on the eve of the Battle of Chancellorsville.*

Grant's Vicksburg Campaign

Vicksburg, Mississippi, situated on bluffs overlooking the nation's greatest river, was one of the two strategically vital cities of the Confederacy (the other being the rail center of Chattanooga). Through Vicksburg poured a stream of food-stuffs, cotton, and other supplies necessary to keep the South alive. If that supply line could be cut off, the Confederacy would begin to wither on the vine, and if the Mississippi were in Union hands, a path was open through the center of the South.

That city became the objective of U S Grant in late October 1862, when he took command of the Federal Department of the Tennessee. A week later, he set his army marching down a rail-road line toward Vicksburg. The advance soon ran into trouble – Confederate cavalry destroyed Grant's supply dump and Nathan Bedford Forrest's men tore up 60 miles of railroad that the Union army needed to resupply. At around the same time, forces under Grant's subordinate William Tecumseh Sherman suffered a bloody repulse in attempting to seize landings north of Vicksburg. That ended Grant's last hope of taking the city with relative speed. He had to face the fact that the Confederacy would do everything in its power to hold on to it.

As winter settled in, Grant faced a most unpromising situa-tion. It had just been proved that he could not simply march to besiege Vicksburg; besides the enemy forces in Mississippi, there was the barrier of swampy land that surrounded the city. But neither would Washington let him and his army spend the winter twiddling their thumbs. He had to get his men doing something. Finally, Grant shifted his base to a point nearly opposite Vicksburg on the western (Louisiana) bank of the river and commenced a series of experiments.

The Federal fleet had already secured most of the major river towns – Memphis to the north, Baton Rouge and New Orleans to the south. For Grant's operations, the Union ships, which were then in the north, had to get downriver past Vicksburg. First, Grant had his army dig a canal so the Federal fleet could bypass the fearsome Vicksburg batteries; the canal turned out to be too shallow to float the ships. At the same time, he sent a corps to try and open a passage from Lake Providence that would put Federal vessels onto the Red River south of Vicks-burg. This operation was abandoned for a more promising one in the Yazoo Pass, 325 miles to the north: cutting through a levee to enter the Tallahatchie River, the Federal fleet made some progress, but a Confederate fort drove the ships away. In the spring, Grant tried the last of his experiments, trying to move the fleet through a tangled mass of streams and back-waters called Steele's Bayou. In that operation, Admiral David Dixon Porter was slowed by felled trees and attacked from the shore by Southerners: Sherman's infantry had to come to the rescue of the fleet, which barely made it back out.

Having tried every conceivable roundabout way to bypass Vicksburg, and with summer coming on, Grant now set a new plan in motion. It was possible because the ground had dried out perhaps just enough to allow his Army of the Tennessee to march south on the Louisiana side of the river. That was one problem. Once the infantry were south of Vicksburg, the Fed-eral fleet would have to ferry them across the river; this meant that Admiral Porter had no choice but to run his ships down-river past the Vicksburg batteries – another problem. Moreover, to mask his troop movement Grant ordered two

Left: *Confederate fortifications around Vicksburg, Mississippi, formed a line about nine miles long. More than 3000 Union soldiers were killed or wounded in the 19 May attempt to take the city by assault.*

Above: *Grant's decision to besiege the city in mid-May ended in the Confederate surrender of 4 July 1863. Food had run out in Vicksburg, and 30,000 Confederate troops – an entire army – filed out to lay down their arms.*

Right: *Skirmishing in the woods around Vicksburg.*

diversionary operations, one by Sherman's corps attacking Haines's Bluff near Vicksburg, the other a cavalry unit raiding through Mississippi: problems number three and four. In short, Grant's strategy consisted of four separate and risky operations involving thousands of men and horses and dozens of ships, all of whom had to work in perfect concert or the entire campaign would be threatened.

The first gamble, running the fleet past the Vicksburg batteries, began just before midnight on 16 April 1863. Admiral Porter's fleet floated quietly downstream, the boilers not fired to prevent telltale sparks. The ships were protected by barges towed alongside and by bales of cotton lashed along the hulls. As the flotilla reached Vicksburg, it was spotted from the shore and the night erupted in flame from Confederate batteries. The Federal fleet put on steam and began the final dash.

A participant described the scene: 'The whole night seemed one terrific roar of cannon. Burning houses made the river almost as light as day. We saw the people in the streets of the town running and gesticulating as if all were mad. . . .Down on the river it was a sheet of flame. One of the steamers and a few of the barges had caught fire and were burning up, the men escaping in lifeboats and by swimming to the western shore. . . . The gunboats trembled from the impact of shot against their sides, and at times the little steamers were caught in the powerful eddies of the river and whirled three times around, right in front of the hot-firing batteries.' In the end the fleet made it through, losing only one ship and a few barges; Porter came to rest at Hard Times, Louisiana, where Grant's army was gathering after their march down the western shore. A few days later, more Union ships ran the batteries.

Sherman then made his feint on Haines's Bluff with equal success: General John C Pemberton, commanding in Vicksburg, was convinced that Sherman's was the main assault on the fortifications. His job done, Sherman marched south to join

Top left: *Union captain David D Porter runs the Confederate batteries at Vicksburg with his flotilla of 18 gunboats, barges and supply ships: April 1863.*

Above: *Eleven of Porter's vessels survive the shore batteries to establish a base below Vicksburg, enabling Grant's army to cross from the west side of the Mississippi to their objective. Three months later Porter was promoted to rear admiral for his services.*

Left: *A panoramic view of the six-week siege of Vicksburg, the key city guarding the river between Memphis and New Orleans. Grant's triumph here was the turning point of the war.*

Grant. Pemberton was further confused when General Benjamin H Grierson's Federal cavalry set off on their diversion, riding south through Mississippi in mid-April and raiding as they went. For over two weeks, Confederate riders tried in vain to round up Grierson. By the time the Yankee horsemen arrived in Baton Rouge, they had accounted for 100 enemy casualties, taken 500 prisoners, destroyed 50 miles of railroad, captured 1000 horses and mules, and taken only 24 casualties of their own. It was a raid worthy of Jeb Stuart, the more remarkable given the Union cavalry's usual ineptitude in that phase of the war.

Now three parts of Grant's four-pronged strategy had come to fruition. The hardest part remained – moving overland in enemy territory to conquer an almost impregnable city, and doing it before Southern reinforcements could reach Pemberton. On 1 May, Grant finished moving his army across the river. At that point, according to orders from Washington, he was not yet to move directly on Vicksburg; he was supposed to march south and join General Nathaniel Banks in attacking Port Hudson on the Mississippi. Only after that town fell were he and Banks to return to Vicksburg together. But upon learning that Banks was busy with the elaborate (and ill-fated) Red River Campaign, Grant made a bold and historic change of plans: he would cut away from his supply and communications lines – something almost never done in warfare – and move east across the state to occupy Jackson, the capital of Mississippi, which would stop enemy reinforcements heading from that direction. Then he would march west and besiege Vicksburg. His army would move with all the supplies they could carry and would forage whatever else they needed from the countryside. With this enormous gamble, Grant violated orders and put both the campaign and his own career on the line.

Sending Sherman to make a feint at Vicksburg, Grant headed west and arrived at Jackson on 13 May. Inside the city were General Joseph E Johnston and 6000 men; they were supposed to be helping Pemberton in Vicksburg, and more Rebel reinforcement were on the way. As the Yankees gathered around the city, Johnston wrote to Pemberton ordering him to cut Grant's communications and then attack from the rear. The Vicksburg commander wasted a day marching his forces around trying to find Grant's supply line: it did not occur to him that there was no such line. By the time Pemberton gave up and marched east to attack, the city of Jackson had fallen to Grant, who then sent a detachment to meet Pemberton.

The Confederates ran into two divisions of Grant's army at Champion's Hill, and the biggest battle of the campaign broke out between 29,000 Federals and Pemberton's 22,000 men. After hours of heavy but indecisive fighting, the Yankees closed in on the only Southern road of retreat and Pemberton pulled his forces back toward the city. It was a fatal mistake – the Confederate commander should have marched to join Johnston in operating against Grant; by pulling into Vicksburg, Pemberton left himself vulnerable to a siege, the outcome of which was virtually inevitable.

On 18 May, Grant and Sherman stood looking at the defenses of Vicksburg. As Sherman generously observed to his old friend, Grant had already mounted one of the most complex and brilliant campaigns in military history. But they still had to take the city. Its fortifications made a line nine miles long, with nine forts as strongpoints; broken ground in the area also worked to the advantage of the Confederates. Nevertheless, Grant mounted a full-scale assault on 19 May, which gained only a few yards. Impatient with the prospect of a siege, he ordered another attempt a few days later; while getting nowhere, the Federals lost 3200 casualties to Pemberton's 500. Grant would later admit that the assaults on Vicksburg were costly mistakes.

The Federals then settled into a siege, gradually extending their lines around the city. It was a nasty business for all concerned. Inside Vicksburg, soldiers and civilians dug into the

Top: *Union soldiers charge into the breach created by an explosion on Fort Hill, one of Vicksburg's nine strongpoints.*

Above: *Taking the flag to the heights around Vicksburg.*

Right: *Lieutenant General John C Pemberton, in command at Vicksburg, discusses terms of surrender with U S Grant on 3 July 1863.*

Following pages: *The battle of Port Hudson, Louisiana, the last Confederate bastion on the Mississippi.*

hills to escape incessant shelling from Union batteries and gunboats. They ate all the beef, then the horses and mules, then went hunting for rats. Both blue- and gray-clad sharpshooters were waiting to pick off anyone who stuck his head out of the trenches. All the same, with opposing lines only yards apart in some places, combatants often passed the time shouting news and jokes back and forth, and bands serenaded both sides.

It was only a question of time, and the time came on 3 July 1863: white flags appeared on the ramparts of Vicksburg. Pemberton and Grant, who were old army acquaintances like so many Civil War commanders, sat on a hillside and came to terms. The Confederates would surrender on 4 July, Independence Day, and Grant would parole them until they could be exchanged, rather than packing them off to prison (such paroling was common early in the war).

For the second time, Grant had captured an entire enemy army. On the 4th, 30,000 ragged and hungry Rebels filed out of the city. Grant forbade any demonstration of triumph by his troops. Far to the east, the Confederacy had lost another critical battle in those days, at Gettysburg, but it was in Vicksburg that the war was really decided. After Port Hudson fell to Banks on 8 July, the Mississippi belonged to the Union and the South was broken in two. In Washington, a relieved Lincoln wrote, 'The Father of Waters runs unvexed to the sea.'

The Battle of Gettysburg

Soon after his defeat of Hooker at Chancellorsville, Lee decided again to invade the North. There were a host of apparently good reasons for his decision. The situation in the Confederacy was bad and getting worse: Grant was about to secure Vicksburg for the Union, inflation was running wild in the South, badly needed European recognition had not come, the Confederate government was torn by partisan squabbles, the Union blockade was growing steadily more effective, and antiwar sentiment was fading in the North. A major Confederate victory on Northern soil might improve all those conditions. And after their string of victories, Lee and his army believed they could whip anybody.

General James Longstreet, Lee's second in command since the death of Jackson, was against the invasion from the beginning. Longstreet begged his commander to pursue a defensive strategy in Virginia and to send troops to reinforce Bragg in

Tennessee; this might compel Grant to strip forces away from Vicksburg to reinforce Rosecrans. Longstreet's ideas made sense, but Lee was set on his plan; offense was his style, not defense, and as with his previous invasion, he wanted to take the fighting out of his home state. The disagreement between the two presaged trouble, and trouble would come in abundance.

In early June 1863, the Army of Northern Virginia pulled away from Fredericksburg and headed for Pennsylvania. It was stronger than ever – 89,000 men, whose spirits had never been higher. The Federal Army of the Potomac was still commanded by General Joseph Hooker, but after his humiliation at Chancellorsville, Washington was trying to find a politically agreeable way of giving him the boot. Hooker put his men on the march, shadowing Lee: the two great armies moved to the northwest

on parallel roads, neither quite sure where the other was, the opposing cavalries fighting a running series of skirmishes that kept Jeb Stuart's scouts at a distance.

That was not good enough for Lee. The cavalry were his eyes; he had to know exactly where the enemy was. In an order that was ambiguous in its import, Lee told Stuart to take out the cavalry and assess enemy strength and position. Interpreting the order as an opportunity to ride around the Army of the Potomac again, Stuart had to detour ever more widely to circle the scattered Union forces. In the end, he would be gone for 10 days, not returning until a battle was in progress. With Stuart gone, Lee was marching blind in enemy territory and would stumble into a fight at a time and place not of his choosing.

On 28 June, Washington countermanded an order of Hooker's, hoping he would resign at this blow to his authority,

Left: *A caisson team struggles in terror amid the thunderous gunfire at Gettysburg, scene of the greatest battle ever fought in the Western Hemisphere.*

Above: *Confederate General James Longstreet, who became Lee's second in command after the death of Stonewall Jackson and fought throughout the war.*

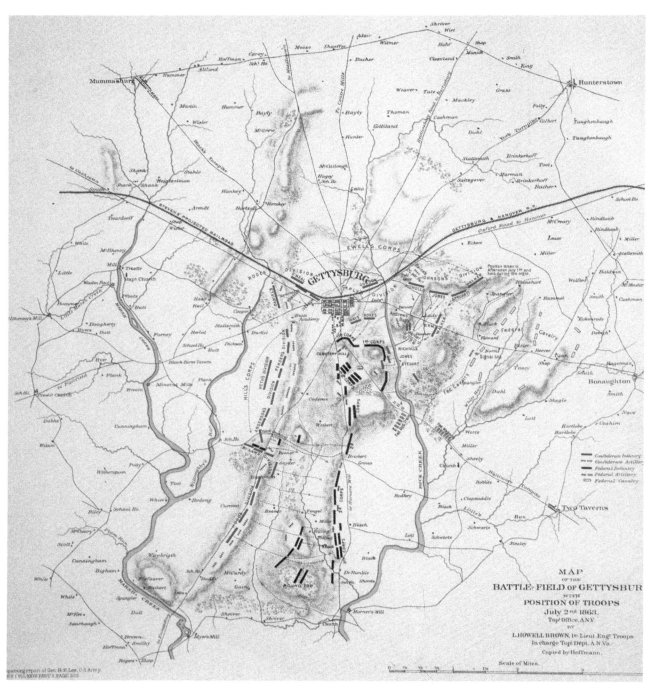

Left: *Map of the battlefield at Gettysburg, Pennsylvania, showing the principal positions occupied by both sides.*

Below left: *Casualties in the three-day struggle at Gettysburg totaled a staggering 28,063 Confederates killed, wounded, or missing in action and 23,049 for the Union. Some 163,000 troops were engaged, 75,000 for the South and 88,289 for the North.*

Left: *The disastrous 'Pickett's Charge' at Bloody Angle: 3 July 1863.*

Below: *Union forces were strung out in a line from Culp's Hill to Big Round Top and Devil's Den when they confronted the Confederate advance of 3 July, which ended in furious hand-to-hand combat.*

ners slowly pushed the I Corps back to Seminary Ridge; Reynolds stayed firm, making sure his pullback did not become a rout – until a sharpshooter's bullet knocked him dead from the saddle.

The fighting escalated steadily, the Union line shaky, the commanders of both sides desperately hurrying men into position. As at Chancellorsville, the luckless Union XI Corps was hit by a flank attack; they fled into the town, where hundreds were killed or captured. By evening, the Federals had been driven from their original line in the west to a position south of town, on Cemetery Ridge. Amid the graves on Cemetery Hill, a Union reserve artillery battery had been placed, for no particular reason. Just before dusk, General Richard Ewell stood across the way: Lee had asked him to assault Cemetery Hill if possible. Seeing the artillery there, Ewell finally decided that it was not possible. Had he attacked, he would have found the position weak and might have changed the course of American history: the artillery position on Cemetery Hill was to become the foundation of a strong Union line.

The situation was beyond the kind of control Lee was accustomed to, but his Army of Northern Virginia had still clearly won the first day's battle. Lee decided that on the next day he would unleash everything he had. Over the protests of Longstreet, who realized that the Union defensive positions on high ground were formidable, Lee ordered a major assault at dawn on the Federal left flank, at Round Top and Little Round Top;

and the general did as hoped. The new commander – appointed over his own protest – was General George Gordon Meade. Irascible, prematurely aged, tormented by a wound from the previous year, Meade was oppressed by the responsibility that fell upon his shoulders. Nonetheless, he was the best commander the Army of the Potomac had ever had, a methodical and tenacious leader with long experience. Hearing the news, Lee prophesied accurately, 'General Meade will make no blunder on my front.' Meade's appointment came almost on the eve of battle; by coincidence, both commanders had decided to concentrate their forces at the same sleepy little Pennsylvania town with convenient road crossings: Gettysburg.

On 1 July, Federal cavalry commander John Buford was scouting there with his 2500 men. Looking out from the west of town, he suddenly saw a column of enemy troops appear on the road, heading in his direction. They were a division of A P Hill's corps; legend says they were looking for new shoes in town. Buford did not have nearly as many men as the Confederates, but he did have some new Spencer repeating carbines (most of the guns on both sides were muzzle-loading rifles). The troopers deployed in a thin line and began taking potshots, the Confederates returned fire, and the greatest battle ever fought on American soil began by accident.

By midmorning, Southern troops were pouring in from every direction. Union General John Reynolds (whom many thought should have been given overall command instead of Meade) arrived to take stock and sent back for his I Corps to hurry to the front; they soon arrived to take over from Buford's exhausted cavalrymen. As the fighting heated up, the Souther-

Far left: *Confederate General George Pickett was unjustly blamed for the ill-fated charge at Gettysburg that had actually been led by General Longstreet.*

Below: *A British-made 150lb Armstrong gun with reinforced breech and barrel.*

Right: *The dour General George Meade led the Army of the Potomac to victory at Gettysburg, proving that it was a redoubtable fighting machine with the right commander.*

Following pages: *A montage of scenes from the epic Battle of Gettysburg.*

Longstreet was to lead the attack. Ewell was ordered to support with a diversion at Culp's Hill to the north. Meanwhile, that night, Meade carefully arranged his forces in a line moving up Cemetery Ridge and curling around Culp's Hill.

Next day, nothing went as planned. Instead of attacking at dawn, Longstreet delayed into the afternoon; Ewell made only a few timid probes at Culp's Hill. However, General Daniel Sickles nearly lost everything for the Union when he moved his III Corps out of position on the Federal left flank and tried to attack enemy troops around the Peach Orchard. Sickles' men ran into Longstreet's guns, which ripped the corps to shreds. Soon after,

Confederates began moving toward Little Round Top, which happened to be the linchpin of the entire Union line.

Federal General Gouverneur K Warren arrived on the rocky hillock of Little Round Top and saw to his horror that hundreds of Confederates were heading up the hill, on which there were almost no defenders. If the enemy secured the hill, they could threaten the rear and roll back the Union line like a rug. At the last minute, a few cannon arrived to slow the advance, but the matter was decided by the arrival of 350 men of the 20th Maine, under young Colonel Joshua Chamberlain (who had been teaching rhetoric at Bowdoin College the year before). Chamberlain's troops shot up all their ammunition and then mounted a bayonet charge that sent the Confederates fleeing back down the hill. The men of Maine had saved the Army of the Potomac.

A day of inconclusive fighting ended with minor engagements on the middle and right of the Federal position. In one encounter in the center, a Confederate column marched almost into Union lines before they were detected; a Minnesota brigade lost all but 47 of its 262 men driving the enemy column back. The Union line had been shaken that second day at Gettysburg, and Sickles' III Corps had been devastated after his foolish maneuver, but the line had held. As Lee had always done, Union commanders had been able for the first time to shift their forces around to where they were needed most. That new tactical effectiveness was to become even more significant the next day. Most importantly, the Army of the Potomac had showed that when their generals were doing their job, they could fight as well as anyone could ask.

Opening engagement.

Position on the 3rd and 4th July.

Retiring with prolonge.

out.

Leaving the field, July 5th.

That night, Meade held a council of war, taking the unusual step of asking his generals to vote on whether the Army of the Potomac should retreat, attack, or wait to receive Lee's attack. The vote was nearly unanimous for the latter. The third day began with a brief but bloody assault by Ewell on Culp's Hill, which was easily repulsed. Then the battlefield was quiet again. As the Union men watched from Cemetery Ridge, Confederate cannon began to appear opposite them on Seminary Ridge; finally, there were 150 guns on a line two miles long.

Lee had decided that, after the cannons had weakened the Federals, he would risk everything on a grand charge onto the center of the Union line on Cemetery Ridge. For the last time, Longstreet tried to talk his commander out of such a move, but Lee pointed imperiously with his fist and proclaimed, 'The enemy is there, and I am going to strike him!' History remembers the advance as Pickett's Charge. In fact, General George E Pickett led only one division; Longstreet, to his lasting sorrow, was in command.

At exactly noon, the entire line of Southern cannon roared, sending a rain of fire into the Union positions. It went on for an hour and a half, possibly the heaviest cannonade in history to that time. But the Southern gunners had made a critical error: they were firing a fraction too high, which sent the shells over the Union front to fall in the rear, thus failing to damage the Federal line.

The guns fell silent, and the Northerners rose to their feet to see what was coming: 15,000 men of the Army of Northern Vir-ginia, immaculately dressed, on a front half a mile wide and three ranks deep, flags flying, bands playing, officers galloping up and down, all marching with firm step for the Union line. The world would never see anything quite like it again. It was the last of the old Napoleonic charges, and for all who saw it, those moments were the most magnificent and terrible they would ever witness.

That fact did not impede the Union men in their work of des-truction. When the Confederates came into range, they were met by everything the Federals could throw at them. Ragged holes began to appear in the line as the storm of bullets and shells tore into it; officers and colors fell; the Confederate right flank began to drift; the left flank faltered and gave way. The center pushed on. Finally, a Southern spearhead reached the low stone wall that marked the Union front and leaped over it. They were led by General Lewis Armistead, holding his hat aloft on his sword to show the way. That moment was the high tide of the war for the Confederacy. Then Federal reinforcements arrived and gathered around the Southern spearhead; there were muffled explosions of pointblank firing, the thud of gun-stocks striking flesh, the mournful roar of thousands of men growling like animals amid the cloud of dust and gunsmoke.

Suddenly Armistead was down, mortally wounded, and the gallant Confederate charge of a few moments before turned into a rabble of terrified men, some throwing down their arms and surrendering, others pouring back down the hill. Lee's great gamble had failed: the Battle of Gettysburg was finished.

The next day, 4 July, a downpour washed the blood from the grass. It had been by far the most terrible battle of the war. Of 88,289 Federals on the field, 3155 were killed, 14,529 wounded, and 5365 missing – a total of 23,049 casualties. Of 75,000 engaged for the South, 3903 were killed, 18,735 wounded, 5425 missing, for a total of 28,063 casualties. Lee had lost over a third of his army.

Gettysburg was a monumental battle, but not a decisive one; it was the fall of Vicksburg, Mississippi, that ultimately doomed the Confederacy. And both armies would meet and maul one another again. But Gettysburg would live in history as the great-est battle of the war – the spectacle of its last great charge, the dramatic finality of Lee's defeat, the unprecedented thousands killed and wounded. Over the next century, millions would come to contemplate those uncanny fields and hills. More than any other battle, the epic of Gettysburg would haunt the American soul – as, long ago, the battle for Troy had haunted the Greeks.

Left: *Mobile field headquarters of the* New York Herald, *which employed more than 100 war correspondents.*

Above: *Confederate General Richard S Ewell's troops helped drive the Union line onto Cemetery Ridge during the first day's fighting.*

Below: *A Union 13-inch shell mortar with a weight of 17,000 pounds.*

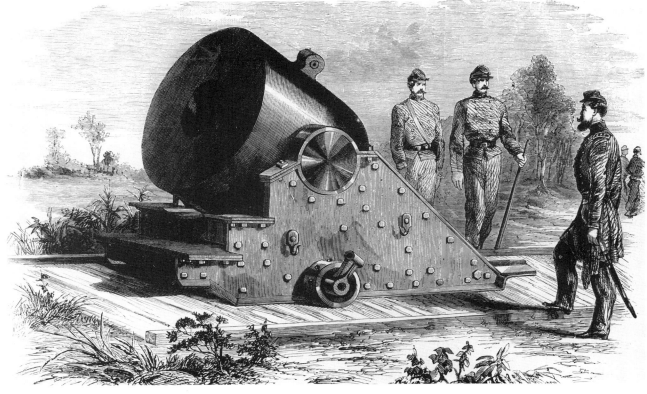

Troubles in the North

If the South had problems with factionalism and unrest in both government and populace, the North had the same troubles on a wider scale. As in the Confederacy, these problems started at the top. Abraham Lincoln had appointed a bipartisan Cabinet full of strong-minded, ambitious men; at least two of them, Secretary of the Treasury Salmon Chase and Secretary of State William Seward, had presidential aspirations. Secretary of War Edwin Stanton was arrogant, argumentative, and inclined to hysterics under pressure; he was also extremely able at his job, as were most of the others. Because of that, Lincoln suffered the piques and power plays of his Cabinet members and depended upon his political skills to keep them in harness. For the most part, he succeeded; Stanton, for example, originally viewed Lincoln contemptuously as a hayseed lawyer, but ended by becoming one of his greatest admirers and supporters. Lincoln also succeeded to a large extent in managing relations with a Con-

gress split between Radical Republicans, for whom Lincoln was a compromiser on slavery and too soft on the South, and Democrats, who tended to want accommodation with the Confederacy and a quick end to the war.

It was harder for Lincoln to ride herd over public sentiment. He assumed almost dictatorial powers, as when he suspended the writ of habeas corpus, but he used those powers with restraint, suppressing dissent only when it seemed genuinely dangerous. An example was the extreme faction of Northern Democrats, called 'Copperheads,' who were pro-Southern and violently opposed to the war. Their primary spokesman was Ohio Congressman Clement Vallandigham, whose fiery oratory kept Washington nervous for months; after losing his House seat in 1862, he became still more vociferous. Then he was sentenced to jail for the duration of the war. Yet Lincoln commuted the sentence and banished Vallandigham to the

Left: *Lincoln and his Cabinet assemble on 1 January 1863 for the adoption of the Emancipation Proclamation, which had been announced the previous September.*

Above: *Clement Vallandigham, leader of the pro-Confederate Northern faction called the Copperheads.*

Right: *The New York City draft riot of July 1863, as depicted in* Leslie's Illustrated Newspaper.

Confederacy. He soon made his way to Canada, from where he ran a campaign for governor of Ohio. Failing in that, he returned to Ohio in defiance of his banishment. Not wishing to give the Copperheads a martyr, Lincoln chose to look the other way. As the war began to wind up in the Union's favor, Vallandigham inevitably lost his constituency.

The Conscription Act, which called for the enlistment of all able-bodied men between the ages of 20 and 45, had a far uglier outcome. The idea of a military draft was widely hated; moreover, there was a provision in the law by which those who could afford it could buy their way out of the draft, or send a substitute. This reinforced many working people's conviction that the conflict was 'a rich man's war and a poor man's fight.'

In New York, resentment boiled over in July 1863, following the first drawing of names for the draft. A mob of over 50,000 people, largely Irish workingmen, swarmed into the city's draft office and set it afire. Their rage then turned against blacks, whom they blamed for the war: during the following days, the mob burned a black orphanage that had been evacuated, torched the office of Horace Greeley's abolitionist newspaper, and beat and killed blacks at random. The rioters also beat a Union colonel to death and assaulted the home of Mayor George Opdyke. By the time Federal troops began to gain control, a dozen people had been killed, and military action accounted for another thousand dead and wounded. Less serious draft riots broke out in Boston and other cities across the East and in Ohio. Altogether, these mob actions were one of the darkest episodes of the war and the worst race riots in American history. It seemed that there was no end to the divisiveness of the war, even within the North and South.

The Battle of Chickamauga

To both Braxton Bragg and his Confederate Army of Tennessee, and William S Rosecrans and his Federal Army of the Cumberland, it was clear that their battle at Stones River had settled nothing; there was going to have to be another one sooner or later. At the beginning of summer 1863, Rosecrans began a new campaign with a strategic coup by feinting at Bragg's left flank. When the Southern general tried to respond, he discovered that two Union corps had gotten behind his right. Bragg had no

choice but to pull back to his next good defensive position, in Chattanooga, the strategic center of the Confederacy because most of the major Southern rail lines met there. (During the Civil War, railroads became a vital element of strategy, moving troops and supplies faster than ever before.)

Concerned over these developments in Tennessee, Richmond took General James Longstreet and his men from Lee's army and dispatched them by rail to reinforce Bragg. Before

Above: *Union General William S Rosecrans held several important commands in the Western theater before he was named head of the Army of the Cumberland.*

Right: *A Northern lieutenant attempts to defend his battery against superior forces along Chickamauga Creek, whose Indian name meant River of Death.*

Longstreet arrived, Rosecrans tried another strategic maneuver to get Bragg out of Chattanooga, diverting the Confederates with troops spread along the Tennessee River and then threatening the rear again. In early September, Bragg pulled his forces from the city and headed south across the mountains into Georgia. Rosecrans naturally concluded that his enemy was running away and sent his army after them.

In fact, the Federals were walking into a trap. Pursuing the supposedly fleeing Rebels, Rosecrans spread out his forces on three rugged mountain roads some 50 miles apart. Meanwhile, Bragg was concentrating his army in Lafayette, Georgia; all he had to do was bring his superior numbers to bear and crush the widely separated Yankee detachments one at a time. But Bragg fumbled his golden opportunity, due mainly to the resistance of his subordinates, who disliked their fractious commander.

Bragg ordered General Leonidas Polk to strike the detachment of Union general George H Thomas; Polk moved in but did not attack. Next day Polk was supposed to hit General Thomas L Crittenden's men; again, nothing happened, and an attack ordered for the 13th was also aborted.

Rosecrans was no fool: the fact that he kept finding parties of Confederates before him, all of whom seemed to be withdrawing toward Lafayette, alerted him that Bragg was concentrating and the Union army was in serious danger. He urgently ordered his three detachments to pull together on the west bank of Chickamauga Creek, near Lafayette. As the Army of the Cumberland arrived at the creek, Bragg was awaiting the imminent arrival of Longstreet's forces, which would give him 65,000 men to a Union force of less than 60,000. He had good reason to be confident of the outcome.

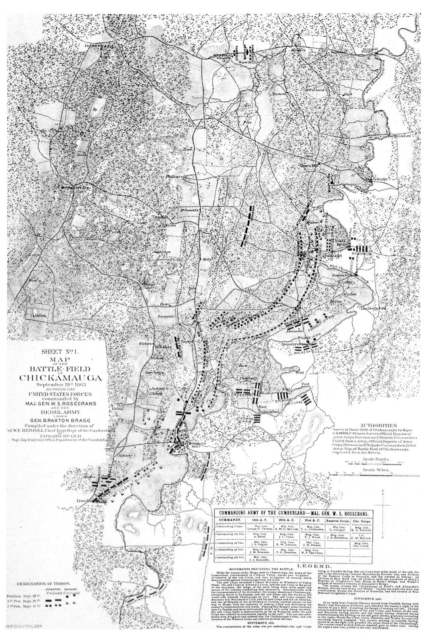

The Southern commander ordered a major attack on 18 September, when the Yankee line was still highly vulnerable. Again, it failed to develop, and Bragg began to bestow new heights of invective upon his subordinates, who had lost him a fine collection of opportunities. For his part, afflicted with violent headaches, Bragg was unwilling or unable to ride to the front and see that his orders were carried out.

By the evening of the 18th, both commanders were in position to fight along Chickamauga Creek, whose Cherokee Indian name meant 'River of Death.' Bragg intended to concentrate his attack on the Union left and try to cut off the Yankees' only path of retreat, a road to Chattanooga. Rosecrans had anticipated this move and made sure his left flank was the strongest. The key position on the left was the steep horseshoe ridge of Snodgrass Hill; commanding there was hard-fighting George H Thomas.

CHANCELLORSVILLE.

GETTYSBURGH.

On the 19th, the Battle of Chickamauga flared when a group of Federal cavalry scouts stumbled across some of Nathan Bedford Forrest's men north of the creek; the Confederates retreated under fire and the infantry pushed forward toward the Union position. Gradually, the shooting spread all down the line. There followed a bloody but disorganized day of fighting, during which a two-mile gap in the Union line between Crittenden and Thomas was never discovered by Bragg. Thomas kept asking Rosecrans for reinforcements and gradually extended the Union left flank to protect the road to Chattanooga. For a time, John B Hood's men (the first of Longstreet's forces to arrive) got onto the road, but Thomas drove them off.

The indecisive fighting ended in late afternoon, and the Union line had held. That evening, Longstreet arrived with the rest of his men, experienced veterans of Lee's army, and Bragg clearly had the upper hand. He ordered Polk to begin at dawn with a strong assault on Thomas at Snodgrass Hill; after Polk's move on the left, the rest of the forces were to join in successively down the line. Meanwhile, across the way, the Federals were busy building log defenses. Rosecrans met with his generals, cautioning them above all to keep closed up to the left. That was the beginning of a chain of coincidences adding up to disaster for the Federal Army of the Cumberland.

At dawn, with a thick fog blanketing the tangle of woods, Bragg sat waiting for the sound of Polk's attack. After an hour of silence, Bragg sent a messenger to inquire after his general, who was discovered having a leisurely breakfast in a farmhouse. Hearing the news, an apoplectic Bragg swore 'in a manner that would have powerfully assisted a mule team in getting up a mountain' and demanded that the attack begin. Polk finally fell onto Thomas, beginning to push the Union left flank back toward the vital road to Chattanooga.

Far left: *Detailed map of the battleground at Chickamauga.*

Left: *The 34-star flag of the Union, from which Lincoln had forbidden the removal of stars representing the Confederate States.*

Right: *Despite his defeat at Chickamauga, students of the Civil War have regarded General Rosecrans as one of the best strategists on either side.*

Left: *A Civil War painting by Samuel J Reader entitled* Last Shot.

Responding to urgent requests from Thomas for more re-inforcements, Rosecrans ordered in General James S Negley's reserve unit. Confusion began to creep into Union deployments; it was discovered that Negley was actually in line of battle and General Thomas J Wood in reserve, where Negley was thought to be. As Negley's men were pulled out and sent to Thomas, and Wood moved into line of battle on the right, the confusion snowballed. Negley and his men got lost, wandering over to Rossville; meanwhile, Rosecrans assumed that Negley was in position with Thomas.

These problems in deployment came to a head when an excited scout arrived to tell Rosecrans that there was a gap in the Federal line between the divisions of Wood and Reynolds. To seal that gap, Rosecrans sent an order to Wood to 'close up on and support' Reynolds. This befuddled Wood, for the simple reason that the scout had been wrong. The arrangement was Wood/John Brannan/Reynolds, just as it was supposed to be; the trees, brush, and fog were so thick that the scout had not seen Brannen's division and assumed there was a gap there. Wood decided that Rosecrans meant for him to pull out of line and march behind Brannan to join Reynolds. Thus, as he pulled his troops out, Wood created a genuine gap in the Union line. And opposite that gap, in the Southern lines – apparently by sheer coincidence – Longstreet was ready at that moment to attack. A column of screaming Confederates charged right into the gap, wheeled to the north, and in short order sent the entire Union right wing fleeing up the road to Chattanooga. During the rout the North lost thousands in casualties and captured men. Among those retreating was Rosecrans, who ran into Negley and concluded, incorrectly, that Negley had been with Thomas and thus that the left wing had broken as well. In a panic, Rosecrans continued on to Chattanooga.

Rosecrans was wrong: the entire Union army had not been routed. At Snodgrass Hill, General Thomas was holding on. While Confederates swarmed around him, Thomas walked back and forth encouraging his men, and they fought like devils, aided by the steep slopes of the hill. But when ammunition ran low in late afternoon, it looked like the end; Thomas ordered his men to fix bayonets, which was the final desperation. Then, at the last possible minute, Thomas saw a column approaching his rear. If those troops were Confederate, he was doomed. They turned out to be the Union Reserve Corps under General Gordon Granger, who had violated Rosecrans's original orders to stay put and marched to reinforce Thomas. Granger's men and ammunition began pouring in, and Thomas kept fighting; only after dark did he make an orderly withdrawal to Chattanooga. The Confederates had won the field, but Thomas was the hero of the battle: forever after he would be 'The Rock of Chickamauga.'

Losses in the battle were among the worst of the war: of 58,222 Federals engaged, there were 1657 killed and 9756 wounded; of 66,326 Confederates, 2312 were dead and 14,674 wounded. Typically, Bragg failed to pursue the fleeing Federals; he seemed unable to believe that he had won. By the time Bragg finally dispatched troops to Chattanooga on 21 September, the Federals were in strong defensive positions. Nonetheless, the Army of the Cumberland was by no means out of trouble: Bragg spread his army around the city and settled down to starve the Yankees out.

Below: *A Currier and Ives lithograph depicting the clash between Rosecrans's forces and Confederate troops commanded by Generals Bragg and Longstreet.*

Below right: *Confederate sharpshooters in the woods around Chickamauga Creek.*

Right: *Confederate General John B Hood is wounded at the battle of Chickamauga. His right leg had to be amputated, but he recovered to fight until the end of the war strapped to his saddle.*

Following pages: *Officers survey the battlefield at Chattanooga.*

The Chattanooga Campaign

On 24 October 1863, General Ulysses S Grant arrived in Chattanooga. Appropriately enough, since he had done more than anyone else to conquer the Mississippi River, Grant had just been named to command the newly formed Federal Military Division of the Mississippi. The route on which he had come to Chattanooga, a tortuous trail from Bridgeport, Alabama, was the only one left open to the Federal Army of the Cumberland, which had been besieged in the city since its defeat at Chickamauga. Grant was to lift that siege and brought with him orders placing General Thomas in command of the Army of the Cumberland and removing Rosecrans, who had been in a state of near shock since the battle. The new commanders faced a daunting challenge. Chattanooga lay in a bowl-shaped depression surrounded by hills and ridges on whose heights Bragg's Confederate Army of Tennessee had dug in and placed dozens of cannon. The Federals in Chattanooga had been on half rations for weeks; their horses were dying of starvation.

Food, not fighting, was the first military objective. Grant immediately issued orders for opening a route along the Tennessee River to bring in provisions – the soldiers would call it the cracker line, after the ubiquitous military biscuit. At the same time, Grant ordered reinforcements to march from Bridgeport, where they had been stuck for two weeks. There were 20,000 men and 3000 horses and mules of Joe Hooker's division. Hooker's men slipped into the city in the middle of the night; meanwhile, Union detachments drove Confederates from positions overlooking the river. On the morning of 30 October, the little ship *Chattanooga* steamed into town with 40,000 rations and tons of animal feed. The cracker line was open, and soon the Yankees would be fit to fight.

A few days later, Confederate president Jefferson Davis unwittingly helped Grant when he ordered Bragg to send 20,000 cavalrymen to join Confederate forces surrounding Knoxville, Tennessee, occupied by a Union army under General Ambrose Burnside. To relieve the pressure on Knoxville, Grant had to attack Bragg soon. Within days, William Tecumseh Sherman had arrived in Chattanooga with 17,000 more men. Despite the growing number of Federals, Bragg remained sanguine about his hilltop positions, assuring an anxious citizen that 'There are not enough Yankees in Chattanooga to come up here. Those are all my prisoners.' It seemed a realistic assessment of the situation.

Grant reorganized his forces and made his plans for battle. On the morning of 23 November, Union cannon rumbled into life, striking the main enemy positions along Missionary Ridge; Rebel guns opened up in reply. Then a new sight diverted the Confederates: marching west out of the city to the sound of bands came 20,000 Federal troops in dress uniform, bayonets gleaming, their ranks perfectly aligned. The defenders figured a parade was underway; surely the Yankees would not be so stupid as to attack uphill into strong fortifications. Suddenly, the parade gave a shout and charged up the slopes, and the Battle of Chattanooga was underway. With no great difficulty, the attackers seized Orchard Knob, a hill between Missionary Ridge and the city that would become Grant's command post.

During the night, Sherman moved his four divisions across the Tennessee River on a pontoon bridge; next day he attacked the northern end of Missionary Ridge. At the same time, Hooker was ordered to make a demonstration on Lookout Mountain, overlooking nearby Georgia. Due to the foggy conditions as

Left: *Generals Grant (center) and George H Thomas (standing right of fireplace) welcome a fellow officer to Thomas's headquarters.*

Above: *For U S Grant, seen here in a famous photograph by Mathew Brady, Chattanooga was the third in a series of major victories.*

Right: *The Union onslaught against Missionary Ridge caused panic among Confederate defenders.*

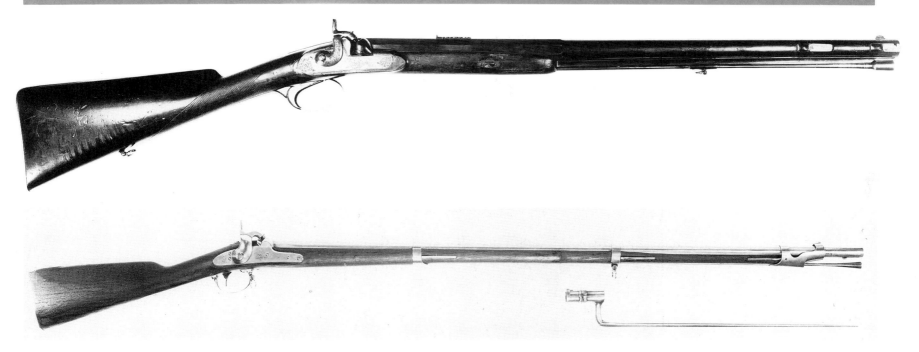

Left: *Chattanooga was important to the Confederacy as a major railway junction. Its loss would split the eastern Confederacy in two by giving the Union access to Georgia and Alabama.*

Below left: *The capture of Lookout Mountain on 24 November 1863 gave the Union control of important high ground and provided impetus for the successful attack on Missionary Ridge the following day.*

Top: *Jefferson Davis's rifle, now in the collection of the Springfield Armory National Historic Site.*

Above: *The Springfield .69 caliber rifle musket was an important weapon of the war.*

Right: *A cutaway view of Warner's Carbine, patented in 1864.*

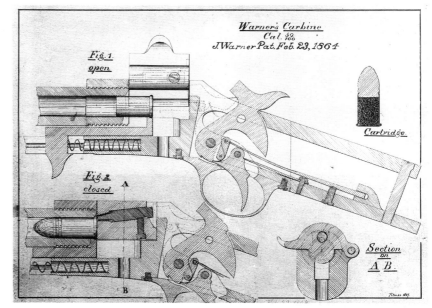

Hooker made his advance, the engagement would be dubbed 'the Battle Above the Clouds.' In fact, it was hardly a battle; there were only a few Confederates on the mountain and they were easily driven away. On the Federal left wing, Sherman had less luck: seizing enemy outposts on what his map told him was the northern end of Missionary Ridge, he discovered that he was on an outlying hill with a ravine blocking the way to the ridge itself.

Dawn on 25 November revealed the Stars and Stripes flying from the summit of Lookout Mountain. Down in the city, the Yankees cheered amid their preparations for battle. Grant had ordered the attack along Missionary Ridge to begin on both wings; Hooker and Sherman set out as ordered, but both soon bogged down under heavy enemy resistance. After hours of indecisive fighting, Grant ordered Thomas's men to advance on the center of the ridge, the heart of Confederate strength.

On the face of it, the order was ill-advised (a similar attack of Grant's later at Cold Harbor would have disastrous results). This time, however, Bragg had prepared the way for his own defeat: not only had he let the Yankees in Chattanooga open up a supply line and bring in nearly 40,000 reinforcements, he had allowed President Davis to strip away his cavalry. And Southern artillerymen had placed their cannon on top of the ridge, where they could not be aimed down the slopes. Finally, and equally importantly, the Federals were in great spirits, ready to follow Grant and Thomas anywhere, while Bragg's officers and men were weary of their testy and inefficient commander.

All those chickens came to roost as Grant's men moved up the slopes of Missionary Ridge. Expecting bitter resistance, Grant had made a special point of ordering the men to stop and regroup halfway up the ridge. The Federals quickly overran the lower line of rifle pits and began chasing the enemy up the slopes; soon the pursuers were only a few yards behind the Confederates, and the defenders farther up could not fire for fear of hitting their own men. Realizing that, the Yankees had no intention of stopping to regroup; their safest position was closest to the backs of the fleeing Confederates. As they charged, the Union men began to shout 'Chickamauga!' Their revenge was at hand.

Watching from Orchard Knob, Grant could not see the details of the attack and was furious that the men did not regroup as directed. He demanded of Thomas, 'Who ordered those men up the hill?' Thomas replied that they must have ordered themselves. 'Someone will suffer for it, if it turns out badly,' Grant growled.

It turned out magnificently – one of the most spectacular charges of its kind in military history. The Federal attack flowed unimpeded right up to the crest of Missionary Ridge, into the teeth of the enemy, who in the last moments were desperately hurling rocks at the oncoming Yankees. Then thousands of panic-stricken Confederates turned and hightailed it for Georgia. Bragg himself barely escaped capture.

Casualties were relatively low for such a major battle – although that made little difference to the dead. Union forces lost 5824 of 56,359 effectives from all causes; the South lost 6667 of 64,165 engaged. After his important, if accidental, victory at Chickamauga, Bragg had let advantage slip into disaster. For Grant, the Battle of Chattanooga was his third brilliant victory in a row; before long he would be getting an important message from Washington. When he next took the field, however, his opponent would not be the relatively hapless kind of general he had come up against so far: it would be one of the Confederate's leading generals, Robert E Lee.

The Gettysburg Address

In early November 1863 Lincoln was invited to make 'a few appropriate remarks' at the dedication of a cemetery for Union and Confederate dead at Gettysburg. The main address was to be given by orator and statesman Edward Everett. Something in the idea stirred Lincoln, and perhaps he wanted a chance to get out of Washington for a few days; he accepted the invitation.

Legend says that he wrote his speech on the back of an envelope during the train trip to Gettysburg. Like most such stories, this one is apocryphal. Lincoln labored over the speech in Washington and polished it until the last minute, with the help of Secretary of State Seward. Clearly, the president wanted to make an important statement. It was the beginning of his public examination of what the war meant and what conceivable good might come of it.

At the ceremony, Edward Everett gave a flowery two-hour oration full of learned allusions, examining the Battle of Gettysburg and the events that had led up to it. Many felt that this was the greatest address of Everett's long and celebrated career. Then, more or less as a ceremonial conclusion, Lincoln stood and in his high, unimpressive voice gave what he called his 'little speech':

'Four score and seven years ago our fathers brought forth, upon this continent, a new nation, conceived in Liberty, and dedicated to the proposition that all men are created equal.

'Now we are engaged in a great civil war, testing whether that nation, or any nation, so conceived, and so dedicated, can long endure. We are met here on a great battlefield of that war. We have come to dedicate a portion of it as a final resting place for those who here gave their lives that that nation might live. It is altogether fitting and proper that we should do this.

'But in a larger sense we can not dedicate – we can not consecrate – we can not hallow – this ground. The brave men, living and dead, who struggled here, have consecrated it, far above our poor power to add or detract. The world will little

Above: *The renowned orator Edward Everett, who spoke before Lincoln at the dedication of the cemetery at Gettysburg.*

Right: *President Lincoln makes his unforgettable address to the crowd gathered at Gettysburg: 19 November 1863.*

note, nor long remember, what we say here, but can never forget what they did here. It is for us, the living, rather to be dedicated here to the unfinished work which they have, thus far, so nobly carried on. It is rather for us to be here dedicated to the great task remaining before us – that from these honored dead we take increased devotion to that cause for which they here gave the last full measure of devotion – that we here highly resolve that these dead shall not have died in vain; that this nation shall have a new birth of freedom; and that this government of the people, by the people, for the people, shall not perish from the earth.'

After Lincoln spoke, there was no applause. He told a friend, 'That speech won't scour. It is a flat failure.' Over the next few days, some opposition newspapers held the speech up to ridicule. Lincoln did receive a gracious note from Everett, who wrote, 'I should be glad if I could flatter myself that I came as near the central idea of the occasion in two hours as you did in

two minutes.' Perhaps it was inevitable that no one at the time could see clearly that these few sentences would err only in the words 'the world will little note, nor long remember, what we say here.' They would be remembered as one of the most perfect and moving utterances in history.

The Gettysburg Address was a prophetic statement as well. Lincoln saw the war as a struggle for the survival of democracy itself: *Can* human beings govern themselves? Is democracy possible at all? If the country remained divided and slavery persisted, then perhaps the American experiment, which Lincoln considered the greatest hope of the world, was indeed a failure. But if the nation survived its tragic convulsion and left slavery behind, it would have proved the value of the American idea and made it stronger than ever; that was the 'new birth of freedom.' And in the end – however tenuously and incompletely – that new birth would come to pass despite years of enmity and bloodshed.

PART 4

The Slow Collapse of the South

The Kilpatrick-Dahlgren Raid

As 1864 arrived, the Union had effectively won the war with three decisive victories – at Vicksburg, Gettysburg, and Chattanooga. What remained was the long and bloody struggle to convince the South of that fact. Many dreamed of some strategic masterstroke that would achieve a quick and fatal blow against the Confederacy, perhaps at Richmond, the capital. Among the dreamers was an impetuous young Army of the Potomac cavalry general named Judson Kilpatrick. His hard-driving style was not universally admired: around the army he was known as 'Kill-cavalry.' But Philip Sheridan, under whom he would serve, summed up his advantages when he said, 'I know Kilpatrick is a hell of a damned fool, but I want just that sort of man to command my cavalry.'

In February 1864, Kilpatrick went to Lincoln with a plan for a raid into Richmond, in which Federal cavalry would try to create such consternation that they could seize the government, release Federal prisoners, and distribute amnesty proclamations, all of which might precipitate the collapse of the Confederacy. For some reason – perhaps because they thought it was just crazy enough to work – Lincoln and the high command approved the plan.

Kilpatrick left on 28 February with 3584 cavalrymen, slipping past Lee's scouts and heading for Richmond in two wings, to catch the city in a pincers. Commanding the advance wing was 22-year-old Colonel Ulric Dahlgren, whose father was an admiral in the Navy. With little trouble, Kilpatrick's wing reached the defenses north of the city; there he took a good look at the fortifications and abruptly thought better of the whole business. Kilpatrick turned his men for home and left Dahlgren to his fate.

Pursued hotly by the enemy, Dahlgren and his men pushed on. Within three miles of the city, they were hit by an attack that reduced them to 100 riders. In heavy rain during the middle of the night, and with Confederate cavalry closing in on him, Dahlgren turned his column north to look for Kilpatrick. The following day he was ambushed and his remaining men captured. Dahlgren himself was shot dead.

The story of the raid did not end there. Papers were found on Dahlgren's body that stated, among other things, 'The city must be destroyed and Jeff Davis and his Cabinet killed.' The South erupted in rage at this planned atrocity, and Lee sent a copy of the papers to Meade with a demand for explanation. The North stonewalled the matter; it has never been discovered whether the papers were authentic and, if so, who, if anyone, had authorized the assassinations of Confederate officials. (If the papers were authentic, Dahlgren had misspelled his own name on them.) Certainly it is unlikely that Lincoln would have ordered such a barbarity. The Kilpatrick-Dahlgren raid remained a mystery and a blot on the honor of the Union Army.

Left: *A Confederate militiaman from Louisiana.*

Right: *Thomas Nast's full-length portrait of Union cavalry general Philip Sheridan.*

Above: *Union Brigadier General Judson Kilpatrick.*

Grant Takes Charge

At a White House reception on 8 March 1864, Lincoln stepped up to a nervous, disheveled-looking officer and inquired, 'This is General Grant, is it?' 'Yes,' Grant replied, and lapsed into awkward silence. The president had just met his new General in Chief of the Armies of the United States. After Grant's series of brilliant victories, Washington had finally settled upon him as the man to whip Robert E Lee and end the war.

Despite Grant's rise from an unpromising West Point cadet and failed Mexican War officer to a destroyer of enemy armies, many remained unconvinced by this shabby, shambling officer. There were plenty of reports about his drinking habits, although no one had ever accused him of fighting a battle drunk. There was also his manner, which was rather reticent for a general: both his face and his personality were unreadable, although he gave an impression of tenacity that led one observer to say, 'He looks as if he had just decided to drive his head through a brick wall and was about to do it.'

Grant had been given an awesome responsibility. Typically, he responded at once by issuing a stream of concise, wide-ranging orders. For the first time, the Union was to have a uni-fied strategy for ending the war. There were to be simultaneous advances on five fronts: Sherman on Atlanta; General Benjamin Butler up the peninsula toward Richmond; General Franz Sigel through the Shenandoah Valley; General Nathaniel Banks on Mobile, Alabama; and a descent by Grant and Meade upon Richmond, during which they were to deal with Lee. In the end, only Grant's and Sherman's part of the plan would make any progress, but that would be enough.

With the reorganized Army of the Potomac, 122,000 strong, Grant and Meade (the latter still nominally in command) crossed the Rapidan River and headed into the Virginia Wilderness on 4 May 1864. It would take just one day for Grant to learn what he was up against.

Below: *An 1865 lithograph of Lincoln with his top commanders, from left, Admirals Porter and Farragut and Generals Sherman, Thomas, Grant and Sheridan.*

Right: *When he became general-in-chief of the Armies of the United States in early 1864, Grant had won a series of crucial battles including Vicksburg and Chattanooga.*

The Battle of the Wilderness

On 5 May, the Army of the Potomac marched into the Virginia Wilderness, scene of the previous year's humiliation at Chancellorsville. The woods were still blanketed by the remains of that battle – charred skeletons, guns, bits of uniforms. The Federals wanted nothing so much as to get out of that terrible place. Lee, however, had no intention of letting them out. He had just over half the strength of his enemy, and the Army of Northern Virginia was half-starved, but his men were still ready to fight any time Lee was. That day they jumped the Yankee column in the middle of the Wilderness. It was the beginning of the most brutal – and the last – campaign of the Civil War.

A Union cannoneer described what developed in the thick woods: '[The fighting] was simply bushwhacking on a grand scale in brush where all formation beyond that of regiments or companies was soon lost . . . I knew a Wisconsin infantryman named Holmes who walked right into the Rebel skirmish line. He surrendered, and a Rebel was sent to the rear with him. In two minutes Holmes and his guard walked right into our own lines, and that in broad daylight. . . . One old fellow was brought up out of the brush. He belonged to the 5th Texas. Some of the boys asked him what he thought of the battle. He was a comical old cuss, and his reply was, 'You Yanks don't call this a battle do you? At Chickamauga there was at least a rear, but here there ain't neither front nor rear. It's all a — — — mess! And our armies ain't nothin' but howlin' mobs!' Accordingly, as evening ended the first day's fighting, nothing had been gained by either side for the thousands already killed and wounded.

During the night, Grant arranged his lines as best he could and ordered a general attack for five o'clock in the morning; before that could get underway, Confederates struck the Union right flank. This was actually a diversion – Lee was waiting for Longstreet to move up and spearhead the main effort on the Union left flank. Soon the fighting had spread along the line, and the superior Union forces drove the Confederates steadily back.

As the Union men pressed forward, they became disorganized, due to the tangled thickets and swamps. For a time, Federal general Winfield Scott Hancock enveloped the weakened forces of A P Hill along the Orange Plank Road. But as Hancock paused to regroup, Longstreet's men made a dramatic appearance, moving up the Plank Road at a trot and pitching into the Yankees. In short order, Hancock was being pushed back. Discovering an unfinished railroad cut that led to Hancock's flank, Longstreet sent his men along it to the attack; they devastated Hancock's forces and were in position to roll up and destroy the entire Union line.

Then fate stepped in: Longstreet was seriously wounded by his own men firing blindly into the woods, some five miles from where the same thing had happened to Stonewall Jackson the year before. As Longstreet was carried from the field, the Southern attack faltered. For several hours there was a lull in the fighting. Grant ordered a new attack on the middle and right of the enemy line for six o'clock. Again, Lee got the jump on him; at 4:15 PM the Confederates pushed forward and claimed part of the breastworks erected by the Federals. A Union participant described that fighting: 'The line of fire . . . ignited the breastworks composed of resinous logs, which soon roared and crackled along their entire length. The men fought the enemy and the flames at the same time. Their hair and beards were singed and their faces blistered. At last, blinded by the smoke and suffocated by the hot breath of the flames . . . they gave way and fell back to the second line.

Meanwhile, repeated attacks by Federals on the north flank had failed to break Confederate positions. In the process, Federal general Sedgwick's corps had drifted off, leaving itself 'in the air.' Late in the afternoon, Gordon's Rebels fell onto Sedgwick's flank and front and again the Army of the Potomac was in mortal danger. Then the coming of night ended Gordon's assault and the battle. In two days of inconclusive fighting in the Wilderness, casualties had been staggering: the North had lost 2246 killed, 12,073 wounded of 101,895 engaged; Confederate casualties were estimated at 7750 of 61,025 engaged. But as darkness fell, the dying was not over: as had happened in the Battle of Chancellorsville, brush fires broke out, consuming some 200 wounded men in the flames.

After their last great battle at Gettysburg, the two devastated armies had spent months in tentative maneuvers. This time, Grant was determined not to let up the pressure: he issued orders to slip around Lee's right flank and resume the advance toward Richmond. Lee, knowing what Grant was likely to do, put his forces on the march to stop the enemy at a road crossing called Spotsylvania.

As the Union men set out, they supposed they were 'on another skedaddle' – retreating as the Army of the Potomac had done before after being battered by Lee. Then the advance reached a crossing and the men were ordered south, toward Richmond, not north in retreat. As Grant appeared at the head of the column, wave after wave of cheers broke out. Longstreet had accurately predicted of Grant, 'That man will fight us every day and every hour till the end of the war.' And the Army of the Potomac was prepared to follow him. Fortunately for them all, they could not imagine the months of incredible suffering and dying that would entail.

Above: *Union General Winfield Scott Hancock, whose troops were overwhelmed by General Longstreet's in the Virginia Wilderness on 5 May 1864.*

Top right: *A double line of Union breastworks.*

Right: *Confederates seize a Union position on the Brock Road.*

Left: Battle artist A R Waud at work in the field.

Below: Waud's sketch of the rescue of wounded Union soldiers from the burning woods of the Wilderness: 6, May 1864. This was the start of the war's last – and most grueling – campaign.

Right: H A Ogden's painting of Grant conferring with two of his officers at the Battle of the Wilderness.

The Battle of Spotsylvania

Dawn of 8 May 1864 found the advance units of the Army of the Potomac en route to Richmond, circling Lee's Army of Northern Virginia. At the road between Todd's Tavern and Spotsylvania, the Yankees were astonished to find a line of Confederates waiting for them. The day before, as Grant had ordered his army on the march after the Battle of the Wilderness, Lee had told one of his officers, 'General Grant is not going to retreat. He will move his army to Spotsylvania. I am so sure of his next move that I have already made arrangements . . . to meet him there.'

Shooting broke out briefly when the Federals reached Spotsylvania, but they were so tired from double-time marching that they could scarcely do more than stumble toward the Confederate line. That night and next day, both armies built strong breastworks – usually a stack of logs with a 'head log' at the top, leaving space beneath to shoot through. There was only light skirmishing on 10 May, but men still died: well back in Union lines, one stray bullet found VI Corps commander John Sedgwick, whose last words were addressed to a dodging soldier: 'They couldn't hit an elephant at this distance.'

Lee's lines followed the shape they had fallen into during the fighting on the 8th – a large, irregular crescent. In the middle was a bulging salient the soldiers dubbed the 'mule shoe'; history would remember it as 'Bloody Angle,' for a sharp turn in the line. The fact that Lee allowed this salient to stand was a peculiar lapse. Salients are notoriously difficult to defend, since attacking forces can hit them on three sides and their arc creates a diverging defensive fire and converging offensive fire.

On 10 May, Grant received an erroneous report that Lee was retreating north and tried to hold the Confederates in position by moving on the Southern left. By no means retreating, Lee sent a detachment that handled the Federals roughly. As dusk approached, a more promising development appeared for the Union when young Colonel Emory Upton convinced Grant to let him take a crack at the salient. Grant gave him a brigade, with which Upton set out at a dead run toward the salient. A spearhead of Federals drove right through a rain of bullets and leapt over the breastworks, some of them pitching in their bayoneted rifles like harpoons; Upton had broken through the very center of the Confederate line. All he needed now were some reinforcements – already on the way – to break Lee's army apart. But a wall of Southern artillery turned back the reinforcements and Upton had to pull back with heavy losses (although he brought 1000 prisoners with him). Grant was impressed by the vulnerability of the salient. 'A brigade today – we'll try a corps tomorrow,' he said.

The morning of 12 May was drizzly and blanketed with fog. Looking out from the salient, General Edward Johnson was worried. The day before, Lee had removed the salient's few cannon to meet a supposed Federal threat on the right. He had promised to have them back in the morning, but the guns had not arrived. Johnson's position had been overrun once already; without cannon and with only 5000 men, he was not sure he could hold on against another attack. As he speculated, he began to hear cheering in the distance. Then out of the fog rolled a wave of 20,000 Yankees, Hancock's entire II Corps. There was no stopping them; despite hundreds of casualties from the blistering Confederate fire, the attackers flowed like a juggernaut right over the breastworks. Johnson saw his cannon arrive at the gallop, only to be engulfed by the enemy; soon Johnson himself was a prisoner. The Army of Northern Virginia was on the verge of final collapse and its reserves were almost exhausted.

Below: *The fight at Spotsylvania Court House (8-12 May), like that in the Wilderness, brought heavy losses to both sides without a clear-cut victory for either army. The Union took 6800 casualties, the* *Confederacy, 5000, in the salient alone, and one soldier described 12 May as 'the most terrible day I have ever lived.' From this point on, it would be Grant vs Lee until the end.*

At that moment Lee was sitting on his horse at the base of the salient, listening in despair. He had heard a frantic burst of fire followed by an ominous silence, and he knew what that meant: the Yankees had broken into the salient and now they were using the bayonet on his men. His army was dying out there in that silence and fog. He spurred his horse to look for General John B Gordon's Virginia reserves. Finding that they were already moving out, Lee rode to the head of the column, clearly intending to lead them into the fight himself, to save his army personally or die in the attempt. Seeing what his commander was doing, Gordon seized Lee's bridle and shouted, 'General Lee, you shall not lead my men! They have never failed you. They will not fail you now!' Soldiers gathered around, their murmers growing to a cadenced shout: 'General Lee to the rear! General Lee to the rear!' They would not let him go before the guns. Lee was virtually carried to the rear, horse and all; as the attack moved out toward the salient, he turned to shout, 'God bless the Virginians!'

The Confederate counterattack fell onto the disorganized Federals in the salient like a thunderclap, driving them back over the breastworks. But there the Yankees stayed; now they had a general who would let them fight, and they were not going to retreat again. For the Confederates, it was a simple equation: the line had to be held or the war was lost. The result at the parapets of Bloody Angle was a day of fighting as nightmarish as anything ever seen in warfare. As one Southern participant remembered it, the horror of that day subdued the usual jaunty tone of war memoirs:

'The battle near the "angle" was probably the most desperate engagement in the history of modern warfare, and presented features which were absolutely appalling. It was chiefly a savage hand-to-hand fight across the breastworks. Rank after rank was riddled by shot and shell and bayonet-thrusts, and finally sank, a mass of torn and mutilated corpses; then fresh troops rushed madly forward to replace the dead, and so the murderous work went on. Guns were run up close to the parapet, and double charges of canister played their part in the bloody work. The fence-rails and logs in the breastworks were shattered into splinters, and trees over a foot and a half in diameter were completely cut in two by the incessant musketry fire . . .

'The opposing flags were in places thrust against each other, and muskets were fired with muzzle against muzzle. Skulls were crushed with clubbed muskets, and men stabbed to death with swords and bayonets thrust between the logs in the parapet which separated the combatants. Wild cheers, savage yells, and frantic shrieks rose above the sighing of the wind and the pattering of the rain, and formed a demoniacal accompaniment to the booming of the guns. . . . Even the darkness of night and the pitiless storm failed to stop the fierce contest, and the deadly strife did not cease till after midnight. Our troops had been under fire for twenty hours, but they still held the position which they had so dearly purchased.'

At three o'clock in the morning, the Confederates pulled back to a new line across the base of the salient, and the Union claimed the ghastly breastworks and their chest-high heaps of dead and wounded. Nearly 7000 Union men had fallen, and probably more Southerners, for the now useless square mile of land within the salient. But the Army of Northern Virginia had survived to fight again.

Skirmishing and maneuvering continued at Spotsylvania for another seven days. Then, on 19 May, Grant tried his 'sidle' again, slipping around Lee's flank toward Richmond. And again, Lee raced to stop the Army of the Potomac.

Above: *A R Waud's sketch of Federal and Southern troops exchanging fire from trenches only yards apart during the fight for Bloody Angle.*

Right: *Robert E Lee was a superb defensive fighter – one of the main reasons that the South held on until 1865.*

Following pages: *At Spotsylvania, Grant showed the relentless determination to fight on regardless of the cost in men and materials that is the hallmark of modern warfare.*

The Death of Jeb Stuart

On the day before Lee's army held the line at Spotsylvania, the South lost another vital element of its ascendancy in Virginia. It was done at the hands of a little Irishman named Phil Sheridan, who had been with Grant at Chattanooga and came East with him to take command of the Army of the Potomac's cavalry. Sheridan was fully as aggressive as Grant and Lee, but in contrast to the mild manners of those two, he acted the part: he was abrasive, a master of expletive, and in battle tore around the field like a whirlwind.

'Little Phil' was also ready to battle his superiors when necessary. In the Army of the Potomac, cavalry had usually been a minor element of strategy, largely wasted on guard duty and protecting the perimeters. Sheridan had declared, 'I'm going to take the cavalry away from the bobtailed brigadier generals'; he intended to make his horsemen a mobile striking force like Jeb Stuart's. That independent attitude, and Sheridan's tactlessness, led to a shouting match with Meade after the race to Spotsylvania – frustrated by Lee's arrival first, an enraged Meade accused the cavalry of obstructing the infantry, and Sheridan replied in kind. Finally, Meade stormed off and told Grant that the cavalryman was so arrogant as to claim his men could whip Jeb Stuart. Ignoring the quarrel, Grant replied, 'Did Sheridan say that? Well, he generally knows what he is talking about. Let him start right out and do it.'

Thus on 9 May, Sheridan and 10,000 troopers set off on the road to Richmond, knowing that the Cavalier was bound to appear somewhere in their path. Two days later, Stuart and 8000 cavalrymen were waiting for them at an abandoned shack called Yellow Tavern, six miles from Richmond. The Rebels expected to send the upstart Yankee troopers running for home, as they had done so many times before.

After some preliminary skirmishes, the first major attack was led by a fearless young Union cavalry general named George Armstrong Custer. His men fell with a will on the Confederate left flank. The fighting developed into a series of charges and countercharges back and forth across the field, the Confederates gradually weakening. During one Union pullback, a dismounted private named J A Huff raised his pistol to take a crack at a nearby enemy officer, who was shooting from horseback and shouting encouragement to his men. Huff's bullet hit home and Jeb Stuart reeled in the saddle. Carried from the field writhing in pain, the Cavalier still had enough fight left to raise himself and shout, 'Go back! Go back! I had rather die than be whipped.'

In the end his men were whipped that day at Yellow Tavern, and Jeb Stuart did die – next day, at the home of his brother-in-law. Of the triumvirate that had led the South to its greatest victories – Lee, Jackson, and Stuart – Lee was now the only one left. Hereafter, Sheridan would lead the Union cavalry on campaigns more destructive than even Stuart had dreamed of.

Below left: *Union Generals Meade, Sedgwick, and Tyler (center) at Brandy Station, Virginia, in 1864.*

Right: *A casualty of the 13th Pennsylvania Regiment – the Bucktails – from a battlefield sketch by Edwin Forbes.*

Below: *Jeb Stuart leads his last cavalry charge at Yellow Tavern, near Richmond, on 9 May 1864.*

Following pages: left, *Grant in the field;* **right,** *a Confederate sharpshooter takes aim.*

The Battle of Cold Harbor

After the battle in the Wilderness that began his campaign against Lee, Grant had written defiantly to Washington, 'I propose to fight it out on this line if it takes all summer.' There would be several lines, however, and it would take more than a summer to run Robert E Lee to ground. Since Spotsylvania had not panned out, Grant repeated his maneuver for the third time, slipping around Lee's right flank in an effort to reach Richmond. As before, Lee anticipated the move and put his army in the way at the North Anna River.

The Southern lines there were in a wedge-shaped formation, and on 23 May 1864, Grant's army attacked and split in half along the wedge. Lee had a rare opportunity to strike his enemy one-half at a time, but at that point he was bedridden with fever and could not direct his forces. After two more days of indecisive fighting along the North Anna, Grant again sidled the Army of the Potomac to the left, flanking Lee, and the Confederates shadowed the move.

On 1 June the Federals found the Army of Northern Virginia entrenched at Cold Harbor and immediately mounted assaults, to no avail. Grant ordered more for the next day, but slow troop movements and rain forced a postponement. Clearly, the Union commander was frustrated; three times now, the vastly outnumbered Confederates had stymied his attacks. This time, Grant was determined to send his army full strength into those enemy breastworks and get it over with once and for all. It was the most disastrous decision he ever made. For their part, the men knew perfectly well what was coming: the night before the battle, soldiers were seen sewing name tags on their clothes, so their bodies could be identified.

The Battle of Cold Harbor on 3 June was complicated in its details, but in essence it was a series of attacks on Confederate positions that were all but invulnerable. The first struck the entire Southern line at 4:30 AM. As the Federals approached, an observer recalled, 'there rang out suddenly on the summer air such a crash of artillery and musketry as is seldom heard in war.' The bluecoats fell in waves. For a few moments they reached the breastworks, but a countercharge drove them back. Within the first half hour of fighting, thousands of Union men dropped before the gray line. Yet after that devastating repulse, Grant ordered a second general assault. It was carried out raggedly, with many troops holding back, and was repulsed again. A third time came the order to attack. This time the troops made no more than a token attempt.

Grant would later write of that day at Cold Harbor, 'I regret this assault more than any one I have ever ordered.' He added, accurately enough, 'No advantage whatever was gained from the heavy loss we sustained.' Another commentator would be more direct: 'Cold Harbor represents a horrible failure of Federal generalship.' Union casualties on 3 June totalled 7000, added to some 5000 suffered on 1 and 2 June; Confederate losses were 8 times smaller – around 1500. And the dying continued after the fighting ended: apparently, neither general was willing to imply that he was beaten by asking for a truce to collect the wounded. As a result, no stretcher parties went out for four days and hundreds of men died, in full view of both lines, of wounds, exposure, and thirst.

In a month of ceaseless marching and fighting, the Army of the Potomac had lost 50,000 casualties, 41 percent of their original strength; Army of Northern Virginia losses had been 32,000, 46 percent of their strength. It was an outrageous price to pay for Grant's doggedness and he knew that as well as anybody. He also knew that his army could find virtually unlimited supplies of cannon fodder in the North; in contrast, the South was near the end of its supply of manpower. Whatever the cost, as long as the Union kept fighting, the outcome was inevitable.

There would be no more battles like Cold Harbor or Spotsylvania; the Union army could not bear that. Grant had tried and failed to hammer Lee into submission. Now, as he had finally done after the disastrous assaults on Vicksburg, Grant would pursue the slow but sure strategy of a siege. This time he turned his army not toward Richmond, but toward its back door – Petersburg.

Left: A Samuel J Reader painting of Confederate horsemen riding into line of battle.

Above: *Carver Hospital for Union veterans in Washington, DC, in 1864, the year that Clara Barton was appointed superintendent of nurses for the Army of the James. After the war ended, she formed and headed a bureau to search for missing men.*

Right: *A grim harvest of death from the battlefield at Cold Harbor, Virginia.*

Top left: *A Louisiana* Tigre *in colorful Oriental garb similar to that of the Zouave troopers of the French Army.*

Above: *Zouaves on night picket duty.*

Top right: *Both North and South fielded colorfully uniformed troopers during the war, although they are usually thought of as the Blue and the Grey.*

Right: *The Union army attempted a frontal assault at Cold Harbor, a few miles north of Richmond, and lost 6000 men in a single hour: 1 June 1864.*

Forrest's War

The old photographs have much to do with how we know the men who led the Civil War. In Grant's face we see – or imagine we see – traces of a man long used to holding at bay desperation and the bottle; in Lee we see the patrician temperament, the avuncular kindness, although nothing of the ruthless fighter that lay beneath these appearances. In Nathan Bedford Forrest we see a lean, steely-eyed Southerner accustomed to success, taking it for granted that his word will be obeyed, and with a simmering potential for violence.

Forrest was a businessman before the war and made a fortune in various pursuits, one of them being slave trading. Thus, unlike most of the war's major figures, he had not learned his tactics and military history in the classrooms of West Point, so he did not fight by the book. Perhaps that is one reason he was so successful a leader in battle; the other reason is simply that he had an instinctive gift for it. (He was not, as legend has it, illiterate. It was simply that his spelling followed the rules no more than did his tactics.)

At the beginning of the war, Forrest did what a lot of zealous rich men did in those days when recruitment and officer selection were informal – he raised and equipped a mounted regiment out of his own pocket and thereby was given the rank of colonel. He fought the Northerners at Fort Donelson, angrily rejected the idea of surrender, and slipped his men out before Grant claimed the fort. At Shiloh, Forrest and his men used shotguns to keep the bluecoats away from the Southern retreat; that day he was shot and the doctors declared the wound fatal, but Forrest was back in the saddle in three weeks.

Forrest was not happy to be attached to the armies of losing generals. Finally, in summer 1862, Richmond made him a brigadier general with an independent command of 1400 men; they took up the raiding business, mostly in Tennessee. By early 1863 they had become a serious threat to Federal operations in the area, repeatedly coming out of nowhere to hit railroads and supply depots of the Army of the Cumberland. General Rosecrans sent out a mounted column of some 1500 men under Colonel Abel Streight to chase Forrest down. Instead, Streight found himself fleeing out of Tennessee and into Alabama, as Forrest ordered his pursuing men to 'Shoot at everything blue and keep up the scare.' After two weeks of that, the exhausted Streight met with Forrest to discuss terms. As they talked, the small Rebel command marched by in the distance – in a circle, convincing Streight that he was outnumbered. When the Union colonel discovered he had surrendered 1466 men to a force of

500, he was more than a little piqued.

It was around that time that Forrest gave one of many demonstrations of his savage temper, courage, and preternatural gift for survival (during the war he had 29 horses shot from under him). One of his officers became so outraged at Forrest's cavalier treatment of him that he pulled a gun and shot his commander. Forrest grabbed the man's pistol hand, held it while he opened a knife with his teeth, and stabbed his assailant. There followed a wild chase, the seriously wounded Forrest bellowing and flourishing the knife as he pursued the mortally wounded officer through the streets. A couple of days later, there was a tearful reconciliation at the officer's deathbed. Forrest himself was soon back in action.

Jefferson Davis never did give Forrest a major command, and despite his success as an independent raider, attached the cavalryman to Bragg's army in Tennessee for a time. When Bragg refused to follow up the victory at Chickamauga with a determined pursuit, Forrest was apoplectic: 'You commenced your cowardly . . . persecution after Shiloh, because I reported to Richmond facts, while you reported damned lies,' he roared to Bragg. 'You robbed me of my command that I armed and equipped from the enemies. You are a coward and a damned scoundrel. You may as well not issue any more orders to me, for I will not obey them.' After that kind of insubordination, there was not much choice but to shoot Forrest or give him back a command. Davis had enough sense to do the latter.

Left: *Confederate cavalry leader Nathan B Forrest defied great odds in surviving the war. Twenty-nine horses were shot from under him.*

Above: *Union General William T Sherman won renown in the North and hatred in the South for his exploits in the war. His military career would continue until 1883, when he retired from the US Army as commander-in-chief.*

Right: *Union Colonel Abel Streight leads a charge on Forrest's guns before his defeat by the Confederate cavalry leader.*

Following pages: *A romaticized postwar painting of the Battle of Kennesaw Mountain, near Marietta, Georgia: 27 June 1864.*

With his new troops, Forrest surrounded Fort Pillow, near Jackson, Tennessee, on 12 April 1864. Displaying his usual tactical brilliance, he established his forces in positions from which they could attack the fort without coming under direct fire. After a request for surrender was declined, they mounted a lightning assault that stormed the ramparts easily. What followed was the worst atrocity of the war.

Half the fort's more than 500 defenders were black troops. The existence of black soldiers in the Union army was controversial in the still-racist North, but it was a cause for violent outrage in the South: at one point it was proposed that captured white Union officers of black troops should be hanged. By the end of the day at Fort Pillow, 200 of the 262 black soldiers were dead, compared to fewer than a hundred whites. Survivors

Left: Forrest leads his men out to attack the Federal right at Brice's Cross Roads, Mississippi.

Below: Confederates storm Fort Pillow, near Jackson, Tennessee, before the infamous massacre of the garrison's black troops.

reported the Confederates shooting surrendered men, shouting, 'No quarter! Kill the damned niggers!' A postwar Northern committee of investigation would cite cases of black prisoners having been set afire and buried alive. Later studies questioned some of these atrocities, but there is still evidence of deliberate massacre. Forrest himself wrote soon after the battle, 'The river was dyed with the blood of the slaughtered for two hundred yards . . . it is hoped that these facts will demonstrate to the Northern people that Negro soldiers cannot cope with Southerners.' (In fact, the record of Northern black troops in the war was outstanding.)

In the spring and summer of 1864, Forrest's particular specialty was harassing the supply lines of General Sherman's operations on Atlanta. Finally, Sherman wrote with his accustomed ferocity, 'That devil Forrest must be hunted down and killed if it costs ten thousand lives and bankrupts the Federal treasury.' Sherman sent General S D Sturgis to do the job.

The military maxim that Forrest gave to history (probably a parody of his actual words) was 'Git thar fustest with the mostest.' In June 1864 he would demonstrate the soundness of that tactical principal when he met Sturgis in the Battle of Brice's Cross Roads, Mississippi. Forrest then commanded 4713 men and had 12 cannon; Sturgis had 3000 cavalry, 4800 infantry, and 18 cannon. Outnumbered as usual, he would be able to mass his troops to gain local superiority and move them to best advantage.

The Confederate advance of 900 men met Sturgis's 3200 cavalry at the cross roads, and the first Southern attacks were so daunting that the Federals halted immediately. Forrest made

sure his men stayed in sight and kept moving; the Yankees never suspected how few their opponents were. As Forrest knew they would, the Union infantry arrived exhausted from marching double time in the summer heat. Forrest massed his troops, now 1700 strong, and broke through the enemy center; then, with his full force, he mounted attacks on both flanks. Before long the Federals were fleeing in panic, Forrest's men chasing them all night and into the next day. With less than half the strength of his enemy, Forrest had captured enormous quantities of supplies and all the Federal cannon, and had inflicted casualties of 227 dead, 394 wounded, and 1623 captured, to total Southern casualties of 492. Brice's Cross Roads was one of the most brilliant Confederate victories of the war, and Sherman had to resign himself to continuing depredations of his supply line by Forrest. (Undoubtedly, this is one reason Sherman would decide to forage off the countryside during his March to the Sea.)

Forrest remained at large until the end of the war. In later years, his luck seemed to desert him. He never recouped his fortune and served for a time as the first Grand Wizard of the notorious Ku Klux Klan. His career as a slave trader and his subsequent treatment of blacks made him a less than noble example of humanity. But as a fighter, he was extraordinary. When asked who had been the war's greatest soldier, General J E Johnston, named Forrest, 'who, had he had the advantages of a thorough military education and training, would have been the great central figure of the Civil War.' By keeping Forrest in small commands, Davis held down the only man who might have been a match for Grant and Sherman in the deep South.

Sherman's Atlanta Campaign

After the fall of Vicksburg and Chattanooga, two vital cities remained to the Confederacy – Richmond and Atlanta, Georgia. In the summer of 1864, Grant was inching painfully toward the capital, while General William Tecumseh Sherman was dispatched to conquer Atlanta, a manufacturing and railroad center in the heart of the South. Sherman commanded 100,000 men of three combined Federal armies: the Army of the Cum- berland under 'Rock of Chickamauga' George H Thomas, the Army of the Ohio under John M Schofield, and the Army of the Tennessee under James B McPherson. Opposing these massive forces were the 62,000-man Confederate Army of Tennessee under J E Johnston, who had restored the troops to fighting trim after Bragg's defeat at Chattanooga, where the South had lost some 6000 men.

Left: *Members of the Construction Corps of US Military Railroads near Chattanooga in 1864.*

Above: *Confederate General Joseph E Johnston was given command of the Army of Tennessee to stop Sherman's march toward Atlanta.*

Sherman put his army on the march south from Chattanooga in early May 1864. Immediately, the campaign took the form it would follow almost to the gates of Atlanta: with their superior numbers, the Federals threatened the flank of Johnston's army at Snake Creek Gap, Georgia, and the Confederate general withdrew to prepared entrenchments at Resaca. After unsuccessful frontal attacks at Resaca, Sherman again threatened the Rebel flank and Johnston withdrew to Cassville; flanked at Allatoona, Johnston withdrew to Dallas, where there was a repeat of the action at Resaca – a failed Federal assault and another successful flanking maneuver. So far, both sides had conducted a masterful campaign. Sherman had pushed the Rebels steadily back, and Johnston had sapped his enemy with orderly withdrawals to prepared positions. The troops had done their work effectively despite daily artillery barrages that had accounted for some 9000 casualties on each side.

Arriving before yet another line of Johnston's defenses at Kennesaw Mountin, Sherman was getting impatient. With every maneuver, Johnston's supply line was becoming shorter and his own was getting longer. And the Federals had Forrest raiding their railroad line as well. Perhaps for that reason, Sherman ordered a major assault uphill onto Kennesaw Mountain on 27 June. That had worked against these same enemy troops at Missionary Ridge; maybe it would work here.

The assault on Kennesaw Mountain turned out a bloody

debacle, with the Federals taking 2000 casualties to the Southerners' 442. One Confederate defender wrote of the fighting, 'All that was necessary was to load and shoot. I will ever think that the reason they did not capture our works was the impossibility of their living men to pass over the bodies of their dead.' A few days later, Sherman resumed his old tactic and sent McPherson around Johnston's flank; the Confederates duly withdrew from Kennesaw Mountain to the banks of the Chattahoochie River, the last defensive position before the massive earthworks of Atlanta.

At that point, Jefferson Davis lost patience with his general's campaign of retreat. He removed Johnston from command and replaced him with hulking General John B Hood, one of the most enthusiastic fighters in the Confederacy – as witnessed by a missing leg and a crippled arm inflicted at Gettysburg and Chickamauga. This change of command was exactly what Sherman had hoped for. Hood was sure to come out fighting: with a little care on the Federal side, he was sure to lose.

Hood made his opening move on 20 July with a ferocious surprise attack on Thomas at Peachtree Creek. Although the Federal commanders had expected something of the kind, they had carelessly allowed Thomas to get out on a limb away from the main body. As a result, in a heavy four-hour engagement Hood nearly cut Thomas off. Finally, the tenacious Federal general found enough artillery to drive the Confederates away.

Undiscouraged, Hood struck McPherson's troops, who were on a wide envelopment aimed at cutting the rail lines into the city, two days later. The Battle of Atlanta got underway when Hood ordered General William Hardee out to hit McPherson's flank. While Hardee's flank attack was being met and repulsed, McPherson himself, riding from Sherman's headquarters to see what the firing was about, ran afoul of some Confederate scouts and was shot dead off his horse. When the body was brought to

him, Sherman wept openly; McPherson had been his protégé and one of the youngest and most brilliant major generals in the Army.

After Hardee's attack bogged down on the Union left, Hood pitched into the enemy center and managed to drive through, capturing two batteries. For a time the Union line wavered, but finally the Yankees brought artillery to bear and savaged the oncoming attackers. An observer described the turning point in the center: 'Two Rebel lines came on exultant and sure of victory. All our artillery was opened upon them. Words cannot describe the awful effects of . . . 17,000 rifles and several batteries of artillery, each gun loaded to the muzzle with grape[shot] and canister. The whole center of the Rebel line was crushed down as a field of wheat through which a tornado had passed. The Rebel column gave way.'

With losses of 8000 men compared to the Federals' 3722, Hood pulled back into the elaborate defenses of the city and Sherman laid siege. In mid-August the Confederate commander sent a large cavalry contingent out to raid the Union supply line. Once again, Sherman turned his opponent's aggressiveness to his own advantage: with Confederate forces depleted by the cavalry raid, he sent Schofield and Thomas to cut the last rail line into Atlanta.

That left Hood with no choice but surrender or flight. On 1 September, his army pulled out of the city to the south. Sherman telegraphed Lincoln, 'Atlanta is ours, and fairly won.' Both men knew that the fall of the city would make the difference in the coming presidential election: until Atlanta fell, Lincoln had been almost certain to lose to his Democratic opponent – and former general – George B McClellan. Instead, Lincoln won reelection by a wide margin. Now Sherman would turn his ruthless attention upon Atlanta, ravaging the city while he decided on his next move.

Left: *A Thomas Nast cartoon assailing the Democratic Convention of 1864 for its commitment to ending the war. The Democratic candidate for president was former general George B McClellan.*

Above: *Sherman's men receive their pay in captured Atlanta before starting their march to the sea.*

Right: *Repeating .58 caliber Union gun nicknamed the 'Old Coffee Mill.'*

The End of the *Alabama*

The naval war was fought not only on the rivers and coasts of the United States, but on the sea as well, although there were few of the great battleship duels of other wars. The Confederacy collected a fleet of vessels – some originally private, others purchased in Europe – to raid Federal shipping on the high seas. The most successful of these commerce raiders was the *Alabama*, under Captain Raphael Semmes. In her two years of marauding she took nearly 60 prizes and captured over six million dollars worth of goods.

The *Alabama* pulled in for repairs at Cherbourg, France, in early June 1864. A few days later, the Federal warship *Kearsarge* made an appearance in the harbor; its captain, John A Winslow, sent a messenger out to Semmes asking for the release of some Union prisoners held on the Confederate raider. The reply was a challenge to duel: accustomed to success, Semmes was confident that his ship could beat the Yankees even though he knew the *Kearsarge* had more men, guns, and speed. Winslow accepted the challenge, and the date was set for 19 June. Word of the impending duel went out, and French citizens began heading for Cherbourg by the thousands. The day of the battle resembled a carnival, with spectators lining the cliffs along the shore, and dozens of private ships circling on the water.

The *Alabama* sailed out in the morning with flags flying, crew in dress uniform, and guns polished, while a French band played Southern tunes from a nearby ship. To the cheers of spectators, the Southern ship loosed the first broadside; the *Kearsarge* was quick to return fire. For a time the ships circled one another, blasting away to no particular effect. A percussion shell struck the *Kearsarge* and lodged inside, but failed to explode – a harbinger of powder problems aboard the *Alabama*. As the battle continued, the superior speed and maneuverability of the *Kearsarge* – and the skill of its gunners – began to tell: bulwarks of the *Alabama* were blown away, the rigging tattered, guns disabled. As the Southern ship began to founder and her fire declined, a shell hit her at the waterline and exploded in the engine room. She began to go under.

Soon the firing stopped, and sailors abandoned the *Alabama*; Captain Semmes dropped his sword over the side and followed it. All were picked up by a nearby British vessel. Then combatants and spectators stood watching as the *Alabama* slid slowly beneath the waves. It was as good an image as any of what was happening to the entire Confederacy in 1864.

Far left: *Raphael Semmes, the Confederacy's most successful naval commander, whose two ships took a great toll of Federal shipping for most of the war.*

Above: *The* Alabama *begins to sink off the coast of France: 19 June 1864.*

Left: *The* Alabama *strikes her colors and surrenders to the USS* Kearsarge, *ending a career in which she had sunk, burned or captured 65 Federal ships.*

The Siege of Petersburg

After the devastating Federal defeat at Cold Harbor, Lee expected Grant to slip around his flank again and march for Richmond. For once, however, Grant outfoxed Lee: on the evening of 12 June 1864, the Federal Army of the Potomac quietly pulled out of position at Cold Harbor and headed for the James River south of Richmond. Their goal was Petersburg, which protected the southern route to the capital and its vital rail lines.

In command at Petersburg was General P G T Beauregard. For the past month he had been keeping at bay the army of General Benjamin Butler, who had been ordered to support Grant by marching toward Richmond from the south. Instead, the inept Union general was thoroughly bottled up on the Peninsula between the York and James Rivers. Beauregard, realizing that Grant was heading for his 5400 defenders with the full Army of the Potomac, began sending desperate messages to Lee, but for some days Lee refused to believe that the Federals had gotten away under his nose.

Thus when Grant ordered General William F Smith to attack Petersburg on 15 June with 16,000 men, the city was at the Federals' mercy. But the attack was bungled. Smith was slow on the march and Federal reinforcements got lost on the way, finally arriving at the city in the evening. An assault was mounted and made good headway as darkness came on. Then, in a decision that probably prolonged the war for nearly a year, Smith ordered his men to break off for the night. The troops knew only too well that they would not have such a chance again. That night around the campfires, one Federal soldier heard 'the most bloodcurdling blasphemy I ever listened to . . . uttered by men who knew they were to be sacrificed on the morrow.' By next morning, Beauregard had pulled nearly 10,000 reinforcements off the Peninsula into Petersburg and Lee had finally realized the threat.

As the Army of the Potomac arrived during the following days, Grant ordered more assaults on the defenses, which proved costly and achieved little. Troops and officers alike, drained by weeks of incessant fighting, fell into despair and dis-

organization. By 18 June, the soldiers were simply going through the motions; said one veteran, 'We are going to run toward the Confederate earthworks and then we are going to run back. We have had enough of assaulting earthworks.' That day, Lee arrived at Petersburg with the Army of Northern Virginia. In his futile assaults on the defenses, Grant had lost over 11,000 casualties.

Petersburg was now virtually impregnable. There would have to be a siege, and it was likely to be a long one. Grant spread his lines east of Petersburg and in subsequent weeks and months extended his stranglehold west around the city. Lee's forces emerged to contest every Federal move.

In July, the hapless General Ambrose E Burnside oversaw the last act of his dismal military career. Under his direction, engineers dug a gigantic mine under the defenses of Petersburg and filled it with powder. When it was touched off on the 30th, the largest explosion in American history sent a geyser of earth, guns, and men into the sky, leaving a trench right into the city—a magnificent opportunity to storm in while the defenders were still in shock. However, black divisions specifically trained to lead the assault were withdrawn at the last minute by Meade, who feared criticism for using black troops on such an experimental operation. Discouraged by that, Burnside was desultory about his dispositions for the attack. The result was that thousands of unprepared troops were shoveled into the crater and ended up literally at the feet of a fired-up enemy; the Union suffered 3748 casualties in that terrible hole before the survivors fled. Legend says that Lincoln summarized the general's final military action thus: 'Only Burnside could have managed such a coup, wringing one last spectacular defeat from the jaws of victory.'

So the siege went on, week after week, Federals dying one by one in the trenches and Confederates on the earthworks, picked off by sharpshooters, mortars, and cannon. During those days someone observed to Grant that the two armies were like the Kilkenny cats that devoured each other tail first. 'Our cat has the longer tail,' said Grant grimly.

Left: *Members of the 48th Pennsylvania mine the Confederate works before Petersburg, Virginia, in mid-July 1864.*

Top right: *Union control of Petersburg was the key that would unlock the door of Richmond.*

Right: *Scene of the disastrous explosion at Petersburg, 30 July – A R Waud sketch.*

Following pages: The Interrupted Game, *a lithograph showing the effects of the mine assault on Union soldiers in the trenches.*

Early's Washington Raid

As Lee lay helpless in Petersburg, he cast about for some maneuver that would force Grant to pull troops from the Union army and weaken the siege. The means to do that appeared when General Jubal Early chased General David Hunter's forces from the Shenandoah Valley and became free for further operations. Lee authorized Early, a grizzled old veteran as wily and resourceful as they came, to cross the Potomac and threaten Washington. Lee knew Grant would have to send reinforcements to the capital.

With 17,000 men, Early headed north at the end of June 1864, brushing away General Franz Sigel's forces at Harpers Ferry before moving into Maryland. Not knowing how few troops Early commanded, or that he had little hope or intention of actually conquering the capital, Washington broke into a panic: clerks and deliverymen were lugging muskets around town. The first Federal detachment to stand in the way of the advancing Confederates comprised 6000 soldiers – most of them green – under General Lew Wallace. They were easily routed, and Early continued on toward Silver Springs, Maryland, on the outskirts of Washington. He arrived there on 11 July.

Richmond and Washington were only a hundred miles apart, and more than once during the war Yankee soldiers had been in sight of the enemy capital. But this was the first time Washing-ton had had Rebels at its gates. Scared as they were, many were curious to get a look at these invaders, including President Lincoln, who rode to Silver Springs with his wife and stood looking out over the parapets of Fort Stevens, squinting at the enemy as bullets flew around him.

At that point Early was planning an attack on the Federal positions; in fact, they were then weak enough to be taken. But upon hearing reports of Federal reinforcements pouring into the city from Grant's army, Early decided that the attack would be unwise – and besides, he had done his intended job of drawing off forces from Grant. Next day, as Early prepared to get out while the getting was good, his men skirmished with the Federals at Fort Stevens. For the second time, Lincoln stood up on the parapet as the firing broke out, a fine target in his tall stovepipe hat; the young Federal officer Oliver Wendell Holmes, Jr, pulled the president back, shouting, 'Get down, you fool!' Lincoln seemed amused.

After a successful raid that had aroused the desired consternation, Jube Early was back in Virginia and heading for the Shenandoah on 14 July. Lee expected that Grant would send more forces from Petersburg to chase Early. Grant would do just that; unfortunately for the South, riding at the head of those forces would be Phil Sheridan.

Right: *Confederate General Jubal Early petrified the residents of Washington with a threat of attack designed mainly to draw off forces from Grant's army.*

Below: *The siege of Petersburg.*

Bottom right: *A pontoon bridge across the Potomac at Georgetown, Washington, DC.*

Sheridan's Valley Campaign

Sheridan and the Army of the Potomac cavalrymen spent most of the early siege months at Petersburg pursuing fruitless raids on Southern rail lines. But Grant was concerned about the continuing presence in Virginia's Shenandoah Valley of Jubal Early and his forces, who before and again after their raid on Washington had cleared the valley of Union troops. The fertile farms of the Shenandoah continued to feed the Confederacy.

In August, Grant gave Sheridan 48,000 troops, a mixture of infantry, cavalry, and artillery, and sent them into the valley. Their secondary objective was to take care of Early and, if possible, raider John Singleton Mosby as well. Their main job was to wreck the farms, burn the crops, confiscate the livestock. If that could be done thoroughly, the South and her armies would begin to starve in earnest.

Sheridan's men set out with a vengeance, pushing into the Shenandoah and leaving a trail of fire and devastation in their wake. On 19 September, they located Early at Winchester and moved to the attack. Unused to leading a combination of mounted troops and infantry, Sheridan nearly let his slippery opponent get away unscratched, but finally the Confederates were in battered and hasty retreat south, with Union cavalry in pursuit. Three days later, Sheridan attacked Early again at Fishers Hill, where the Rebels had dug in strongly. Sheridan hit the flank first and then led a frontal attack bellowing 'Forward everything!' The Confederates were routed again. With Early

apparently chastened, the Federals resumed their progress north, continuing their work of destruction. However, the Confederate commander had no intention of giving up. Collecting men and supplies for a new blow at the Yankees, Early was a bit put out to find that a shipment of cannon was sarcastically labeled, 'For General Sheridan, care of General Early.' But soon his men were nipping at the heels of the Federals, to Sheridan's considerable irritation. After dismissing one of his generals for lack of aggressiveness, Sheridan ordered his cavalry general Alfred Torbert to 'Whip the enemy or be whipped yourself!' Taking the fiery commander at his word, Torbert and his men sent the Rebel cavalry running at Tom's Brook on 9 October; the Yankee riders named the final 20-mile chase the 'Woodstock Races.'

Assuming that he'd ended the threat from Early, Sheridan

Below: *The destruction of Southern supply lines was a major element of Union strategy throughout the war.*

Right: *Sheridan's famous ride from Winchester, Virginia, to Cedar Creek rallied his retreating men and cleared the Shenandoah Valley.*

went off to Washington on 16 October to confer with his superiors. On the way back two days later, he stopped off for the night in Winchester, some 20 miles from where his army was encamped at Cedar Creek, near Middletown. Next morning Sheridan awoke to the sound of firing in the distance. An orderly told him it was sporadic, probably skirmishing, so the general did not hurry overmuch. As the shooting continued, Sheridan mounted his charger Rienzi and took the road in some concern, stopping occasionally to listen to the sound. Close to Cedar Creek, he suddenly realized that the firing was approaching him faster than he was approaching it: that could only mean that his army was retreating under pursuit. At that point, he spurred Rienzi with a will.

Galloping over a rise, Sheridan saw the embodiment of every general's nightmare: his army was in full flight, the fields and roads covered by a tangle of men, horses, and wagons. Early had mounted a surprise attack on the sleeping Federals at Cedar Hill, and the soldiers had bolted out of their camps and run for their lives. Sheridan saw a number of officers and men marching in their underwear; to his satisfaction, though, he noticed that nearly everyone had a rifle in hand. He charged down the road waving his hat, the soldiers breaking into cheers as he rode by; word of his return went out to the far reaches of the scattered army. Some unperturbed veterans had stopped to brew coffee along the road while they waited for orders. As Sheridan roared by, swearing like a demon, men began to kick over their coffeepots, pick up their rifles, and head back to the front. As one officer told his troops, 'We may as well do it now; Sheridan will get it out of us some time.'

Sheridan's ride to Cedar Creek was material for legend and song, and there would be plenty of both, but it was not a matter of riding down the road and mounting an immediate charge. It took over two hours of painstaking work before the Federals were rounded up, formed into line of battle, and ready to advance. Many of Early's men, meanwhile, had foolishly dallied in the captured camps to sample abundant Yankee food and whiskey. When his troops were ready, Sheridan rode all down the battle line shouting, 'We've got the goddamndest twist on them you ever saw!'

The Federals swept out to the attack, and a Confederate victim recalled their approach as 'a dull heavy swelling sound like the roaring of a distant cyclone . . . [Custer's division was] riding furiously across the open field of grass to intercept the Confederates before they crossed . . . The only possibility of saving the rear regiments was in unrestrained flight – every man for himself.' In short order, the Southerners were hightailing it as fast as the Yankees had that morning.

The Battle of Cedar Creek finally ended Jubal Early's power in the Shenandoah. In early March 1865, Custer's cavalrymen wiped out the remains of the Confederate army at Waynesboro; Early and two officers escaped with only 20 men. By that time, Sheridan had completed the sacking of the once-beautiful valley, destroying or confiscating its farms, crops, animals, mills, powder works, barns, tanneries, and railroads. He had failed only in rounding up Mosby. As Grant had ordered, Sheridan had made sure that 'A crow would have to carry its rations if it flew across the valley.' Then he headed back to join Grant in finishing off Robert E Lee and the Army of Northern Virginia.

Below left: *Sherman's men wreck a railroad on their march to the sea. When the war began, the South had only 28 percent of the nation's railroad mileage. By 1865 it had far less.*

Right: *A Union gunner races to save his caisson in the fall of 1864.*

Below: *Confederate raider John S Mosby survived the war, but his colleague John Hunt Morgan, seen here on one of his daring hit-and-run missions, was killed in September 1864.*

The Battle of Mobile Bay

By autumn of 1864, the Confederacy had few ports left: Union naval operations and the blockade had shut them off one by one. Among the last critical ports still open was that of Mobile Bay, Alabama. On 5 August, a Union fleet under Admiral David Farragut steamed toward the bay. The admiral led on his flagship *Hartford*, commanding 14 wooden steamships, which he had ordered lashed together in pairs, and four *Monitor*-class ironclads. The latter were an improvement on the original Union armored ship; they had two turrets with a pilothouse atop each, and a smokestack in the middle. The Southern flotilla defending the bay consisted only of three wooden gunboats and a new ironclad of *Merrimack* type, the *Tennessee*. Outnumbered on the water as they were, the Confederates placed their hopes in two forts guarding the entrance and in a number of 'moored torpedoes' (later called mines) out in the bay.

As Farragut approached, the forts' guns opened up, spewing a deadly rain of shells that damaged but did not stop the attacking ships. Worse soon followed: one of the Union ironclads hit a torpedo and sank immediately with most of its sailors. Shaken by the sight, the men on the other ships were disinclined to continue. From where he stood in the rigging of the *Hartford*, however, the crusty old Farragut roared his immortal words of defiance – 'Damn the torpedoes! Full speed ahead!' (or something to that general effect) – and the ships sailed on into the bay.

Terrified Union sailors could hear torpedoes scraping along the sides of their ships, but no more exploded. For a half hour, they circled the *Tennessee*, firing at close range and shredding the ship's armor; finally, the ironclad foundered and gave up. With the loss of their main battleship, the Confederates had no choice but to surrender. Casualties were unusually high for a naval engagement in the Civil War – the Union lost 319 sailors (including 93 drowned of the ironclad's crew) and the South lost 312 (280 captured). And with Sheridan rampaging in the Shenandoah, the South was losing its last sources of food and supplies.

Near right: *The Confederate national flag (above) and battle flag.*

Center: *The USS* Hartford, *Admiral David Farragut's flagship.*

Far right: *Admiral Farragut (right) confers with an officer aboard the* Hartford.

Julian Scott
1873

Left: *Farragut goes aloft to urge his crew into Mobile Bay: 5 August 1864.*

Above: *Confederate ships defending Mobile Bay included the powerful ironclad ram* Tennessee *and three wooden gunboats commanded by Admiral Franklin Buchanan.*

Right: *Union seamen man their guns during the fight for Mobile Bay, which ended in the capture of a valuable Southern port.*

Hood's Franklin and Nashville Campaign

Confederate General John B Hood was not overendowed with intelligence, but he knew how to fight on the field: from Gettysburg to Chickamauga, he had been one of the most gallant corps commanders in the Confederacy. Aware of this fact, Sherman had allowed Hood to fight himself into losing Atlanta. But even as he retreated from the city, Hood was still looking for some way to regain the initiative. He finally decided to march his army north, around Sherman, and invade Tennessee. If he could conquer Nashville, now occupied by George H Thomas's troops, he might force Sherman to withdraw from Georgia to protect Tennessee.

At Franklin, Tennessee, Hood caught up with General John M Schofield's Federals, who numbered some 32,000 to the Confederates' 38,000. Backed up to the Duck River with no way to cross it, Schofield ordered his men to dig in and wait. On 30 November 1864, Hood struck in his usual determined but ill-considered style: in a repeat of Lee's doomed charge at Gettysburg – but with even less chance of success – the Confederates marched out in a broad front, without artillery preparation, over two miles of open ground toward carefully built enemy barricades. Although they were torn apart on the approach by artillery and rifle fire, a few segments of the advance actually reached and briefly held sections of the Union line, struggling hand-to-hand with the defenders. Otherwise, it was an ungodly slaughter. When Hood finally called off the attack after six hours

Below left: *Union General George H Thomas was not a flamboyant leader, but his steadiness won him the nickname 'the Rock of Chickamauga.'*

Below: *The 125th Regiment of the Illinois Volunteer Infantry encamped at Edgefield, Tennessee, during the Franklin and Nashville campaign. General Thomas made* *his preparations with customary care, and Confederate forces led by John B Hood fell apart.*

Following pages: *Men and horses struggle against the mud in Gilbert Gaul's painting* Bringing up the Guns.

of terrible fighting, the Confederates had lost 6252 casualties, including five generals; Union losses were 2326. But Hood gathered up the rest of his army and continued on to attack 'Rock of Chickamauga' Thomas in Nashville. It was the last and worst of the Confederate general's series of tactical blunders. Thomas waited in the city, organizing his forces with accustomed care, while Grant wired him increasingly imperative orders to attack. As Hood reached Nashville and Thomas was finally ready, an ice storm stalled the Federal offensive again. Exasperated, Grant sent General John A Logan toward Nashville to replace Thomas; before Logan arrived, the ice had melted and the Rock of Chickamauga unleashed his full force on the hopelessly outnumbered Hood.

On the first day's fighting in the Battle of Nashville, the Federals hit one enemy flank and then the other, squeezing the lines together and finally driving the Southerners back. Incredibly, the next day Hood stood and fought on the Brentwood Hills outside the city. Thomas repeated his tactic of the previous day – striking one flank, enveloping the other. This time the Confederate Army of Tennessee broke into pieces, the survivors fleeing as a leaderless mob.

A retreating Confederate soldier passed the hapless Hood, whom he remembered 'pulling his hair with one hand and crying as if his heart would break.' Hood had finally battered his army to death on the Federal juggernaut. Some of his men wandered out to join other armies. Many others returned to their homes and farms; they had fought their best, but for them, the war was over now.

Below: *The Union line at Nashville prepares to attack the Army of Tennessee, which it outnumbers two to one.*

Top right: *The Union Third Brigade charges Confederates led by John B Hood at Nashville: 15 December 1864.*

Bottom right: *The ruins of the Nashville and Chattanooga Railroad bridge.*

Above: *The death of Union General James B McPherson, Army of the Tennessee, at the Battle of Atlanta: 22 July 1864.*

Left: *From left, Generals Sherman, Sheridan, and Grant – the triumvirate that ensured Union victory in 1865.*

Top right: *The fall of Richmond, Virginia, capital of the Confederate States.*

Right: *Sheridan's famous charge at the Battle of Five Forks, Virginia.*

The March to the Sea

As Hood moved into Tennessee, trying to draw the Federal army out of Georgia, General Sherman decided to leave him to Thomas and made a new plan – one that would make him one of the great generals of the war and the most hated man in the long memory of the South. As he had done alongside Grant on the way to Vicksburg, Sherman decided to cut away from his supply line and march across Georgia to Savannah and the sea, in the process foraging from the population and enforcing 'a devastation more or less relentless. I will make Georgia howl.'

Atlanta experienced a foretaste of what was coming. Sherman turned the city into a Federal military camp, commandeered its food, and burned all buildings of possible military importance, along with a good many private homes. Half the inhabitants were evicted, and streams of weeping refugees poured out of the city. To protests from Atlanta officials, Sherman responded imperiously: 'War is cruelty, and you cannot refine it; and those who brought war into our country deserve all the curses and maledictions a people can pour out. . . . You might as well appeal against the thunder-storm as against these terrible hardships of war. They are inevitable, and the only way the people of Atlanta can hope once more to live in peace . . . is to stop the war.'

With 62,000 men, Sherman set out east across Georgia on 16 November 1864, cutting a 50-mile swath of devastation through the state. Not since Europe's Thirty Years' War of the 17th century had such a reign of terror been visited on a civilian population. Sherman described the process of foraging mildly: 'Each brigade commander had authority to detail a company of foragers, usually about fifty men . . . 'This party would be dispatched before daylight and . . . would proceed on foot five or six miles from the route traveled by their brigade, and then visit every plantation and farm within range. They would usually procure a wagon or family carriage, load it with bacon, corn meal, turkeys, chickens, ducks, and everything that could be used as food or forage.'

There was, of course, more to it than that – inevitable when hardened soldiers are turned loose on civilians in enemy terri-

tory. The foragers were derisively dubbed 'Bummers'; soon they took to calling themselves that, with a certain fierce pride. One Yankee officer recalled the aspects Sherman did not mention: 'To enter a house and find the feather bed ripped open, the wardrobes ransacked, chests stripped of all contents . . . and all the corn meal and bacon missing, bed quilts stripped from the beds, the last jar of pickles gone, was no uncommon sight, and one to make a soldier blush with indignation.'

By the time he reached Savannah on 10 December, Sherman had proved that the Confederacy was a hollow shell. Only a few scattered Confederate units and state militia had appeared to try and hold up the marauding invaders. The last Confederate forces evacuated the city on the 21st, and Sherman wired jovially to Lincoln, 'I beg to present you, as a Christmas gift, the city of Savannah.' Now he would turn his army north into South Carolina, on a still more destructive march toward union with Grant at Petersburg. The war would be over before he got there.

For all its apparently haphazard devastation, the March to the Sea had clear military purposes: to destroy the supplies of the Rebel armies, to demoralize the population, to demonstrate the weakness of the Confederacy. Furthermore, there had been few outrages against persons – none of the mass murder visited on civilians by both sides as a matter of normal strategy in World War II. In short, Sherman had done his military duty and had done it brilliantly and with some restraint. But by waging war on civilians, he had created a terrible precedent. Future generations would carry the process to ever-greater heights of violence, in the name of Total War. Sherman was its prophet.

Below: *Map tracing the route of Sherman's advance into northern Georgia.*

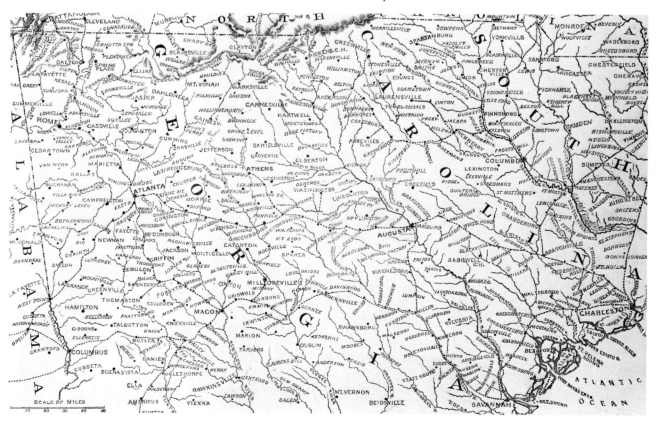

Above: *Kilpatrick's cavalry division is reviewed by Sherman at Marietta, Georgia, November 1864.*

Left: *An engraving depicting the devastation visited on the deep South during the march to the sea.*

Left: *The siege of Petersburg ends in victory for Grant's forces.*

Right: *The ruins of Columbia, South Carolina, after its occupation by Sherman's army.*

Below: *The Confederates burn their navy yard at Savannah, Georgia, to prevent it from falling into Union hands.*

Following pages: *Savannah was one of the few ports left to the Confederacy before Sherman occupied the city on 21 December 1864.*

The End of the Confederacy

On 29 March 1865, Phil Sheridan and a force of infantry and cavalry occupied Dinwiddie Court House, near the last railroad into Petersburg, and prepared to cut the lifeline of the Army of Northern Virginia. By then the Army of the Potomac had closed around most of the city and Lee had failed in an attempt to break through Union lines at Fort Stedman.

Lee sent General George Pickett with 19,000 men to drive Sheridan away, and a desperate battle broke out in heavy rain at Five Forks. Mounted on Rienzi, Sheridan seemed to be all over the field at once, waving his flag, cursing, cajoling, urging his men on against the Confederates. In the end, the Federals captured nearly half of Pickett's force and drove the rest back into Petersburg, where they could not remain now that their supplies were cut off. The next day, Lee informed Jefferson Davis that his army would have to evacuate Petersburg immediately – which doomed Richmond as well. The Federals began shelling Lee's defenses and followed up with an assault that broke through the Southern lines; during the fighting, one of Lee's oldest and greatest partners, A P Hill, was killed. Lee was stricken by the news, but he had no time to grieve.

During the day of 2 April, the Confederate government fled Richmond, as Southern troops blew up factories and munitions works, touching off fires that devastated much of the capital. That night, Lee and his remaining troops made a run for it, slipping out of Petersburg and marching west for Amelia Court House, where Lee hoped to put the men on the Danville Railroad for South Carolina to join forces with J E Johnston. The men of the once-mighty Confederate Army of Northern Virginia were starved and exhausted, and soldiers were deserting by the

Left: *Confederate General Ambrose P Hill, who died in the final assault on Petersburg while trying to get to his troops.*

Below left: *An A R Waud sketch of the Union army crossing the Pamunkey River at Hanover Ferry, Virginia.*

Right: *Confederate officers cross into Richmond by the Potomac bridge to give themselves up: April 1865.*

Below: *The undamaged Confederate capitol building (center) overlooks the ruins of Richmond.*

Left: *General Grant enters the McLean House at Appomattox Court House, Virginia.*

Below: *The surrender document signed by General Robert E Lee and his officers.*

Right: *The two great antagonists part at Appomattox Court House after the Confederate surrender. Grant allowed the Southern cavalrymen to keep their horses and agreed to provide food for Confederate troops. The Union soldiers stood at attention and saluted as Lee left the scene.*

hundreds, but they were still dangerous, and Lee was still in command. Grant and Sheridan knew that he was capable of escaping: they were determined above all to prevent it. Sheridan raced for the Danville Railroad, reaching it on the 4th and thereby cutting off Lee's retreat by rail. The Army of Northern Virginia struggled on, trying now to reach the Shenandoah Valley.

That same day, Abraham Lincoln walked in the streets of Richmond, surrounded by cheering blacks released from slavery into a future with, for the first time, a gleam of hope. The president entered the house of Jefferson Davis and for a few moments sat lost in thought at Davis's desk.

On 5 April, Lee lost Richard Ewell's 8000 men – a third of his army – surrounded and captured by Sheridan at Saylor's Creek. Four days later, as the spent Confederates arrived at Appomattox Court House, Sheridan was blocking the way again. Lee would not go down without a fight. He ordered a cavalry charge that broke through for a moment; then line after line of blue-clad infantry marched in to fill the gap. As the Federals poised for the counterattack, General Joshua Chamberlain (who had saved Little Round Top at Gettysburg) was there to record what happened: 'Suddenly rose to sight . . . a soldierly, young figure, a Confederate staff officer undoubtedly. Now I see the white flag earnestly borne, and its possible purport sweeps before my inner vision like a wraith of morning mist. He comes steadily on, the mysterious form in gray, my mood so whimsically sensitive that I could even smile at the material of the flag – wondering where in either army was found a towel, and one so white. But it bore a mighty message.' Over in the Confederate lines, Lee had just spoken with a great weariness: 'There is nothing left for me to do but go and see General Grant, and I would rather die a thousand deaths.'

They met in the house of a man named McLean, who had moved to Appomattox from Manassas to escape the war, only to have the war come to rest in his parlor. Lee was resplendent in his dress uniform, sash, and sword; Grant arrived in mud-stained field clothes. It was as if neither man wanted to bring up the purpose of their meeting: for a while they chatted idly about the weather and the past, Lee politely pretending to remember Grant from the Mexican War. Finally, Lee asked quietly for the surrender terms. They were discussed briefly, agreed upon, and the document written and signed. Generously, Grant agreed to let Southern cavalrymen keep their horses and to provide food for the Confederate troops. As Lee rode away, the men of the North rose to attention and saluted.

Next day, Lee said his farewell to the Army of Northern Virginia. Then the men lined up to turn in their arms. As they marched by the silent ranks of Federal troops, tearfully dropping rifles, colors, and Confederate flags, Joshua Chamberlain watched, his mind reeling:

'What visions thronged as we looked into each other's eyes! Here pass the men of Antietam, the Bloody Lane, the Sunken Road, the Cornfield, the Burnside Bridge . . . Here come Cobb's Georgia Legion, which held the stone wall on Marye's Heights at Fredericksburg, close before which we piled our dead for breastworks. . . . Now the sad great pageant – Longstreet and his men! What shall we give them for greeting that has not already been spoken in volleys of thunder and written in lines of fire on all the riverbanks of Virginia? . . . Ah, is this Pickett's Division? – this little group left of those who on the lurid last day of Gettysburg breasted level cross-fire and thunderbolts of storm, to be strewn back drifting wrecks, where after that awful, futile, pitiful charge we buried them in graves a furlong wide. . . How could we help falling on our knees, all of us together, and praying God to pity and forgive us all!'

Left: *Confederate soldiers weep as their commander rides away.*

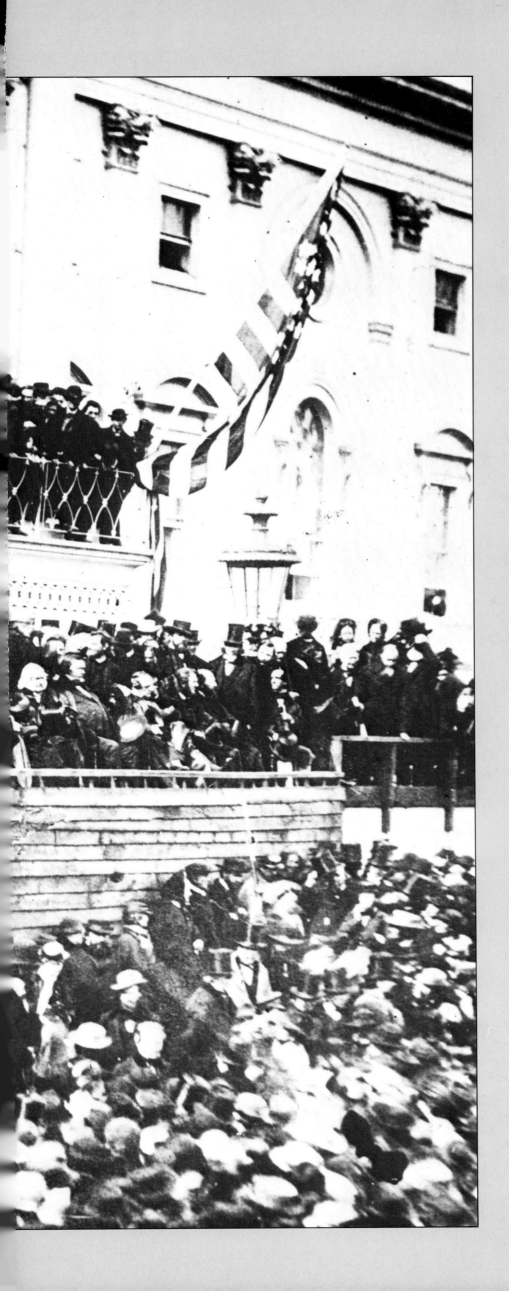

PART 5
The Aftermath

Reconstruction, Relapse, and Reconciliation

It has long been observed that life often has an uncanny resemblance to fiction. When the fanatical Southern patriot John Wilkes Booth assassinated Abraham Lincoln at Ford's Theater on 14 April 1865, he unwittingly wrote a novelist's conclusion to the vast tragedy of the Civil War: Lincoln, who had endured all and held the Union together with such magnificent vision, courage, and skill, became himself the last great martyr to the Union cause.

Of course, the aftershocks of the war did not end there; they will resound as long as the United States exists. As soon as the guns stopped, the monumental problem of Reconstruction arose. Many Southerners knew well that with Lincoln had died his magnanimous vision of that process, which he had proclaimed in his second inaugural address: 'With malice toward none; with charity toward all . . . let us strive on to finish the work we are in; to bind up the nation's wounds . . . to do all which may achieve and cherish a just and a lasting peace, among ourselves, and with all nations.'

That burden now fell to Andrew Johnson, a stalwart Unionist senator from Tennessee who had won the nomination alongside Lincoln not so much because of his ability as because a Southern Democrat on the ticket made for a good balance. As president in a time that would have tested all the wisdom and political prowess of a Lincoln, Johnson proved to be hopelessly out of his depth. The Radical Republicans in Congress, those old unforgiving abolitionists, were more than a match for such a lightweight. The Radicals had fought Lincoln all along for being conciliatory and had dreamed for many a year of wreaking their vengeance on the South; Johnson stood in their way at his peril. Nonetheless, he tried his best to pursue something approaching Lincoln's vision of Reconstruction. For his trouble, he came within one vote of being impeached in the Senate on transparently trumped-up charges.

Previous pages: President Abraham Lincoln takes the oath of office for the second time, 4 March 1865. A few weeks later he was assassinated by John Wilkes Booth at Ford's Theater in Washington.

Above: John Wilkes Booth, the assassin of Abraham Lincoln.

Left: A 'mourning card' for the Confederate States published as a broadside in Philadelphia to celebrate the war's end.

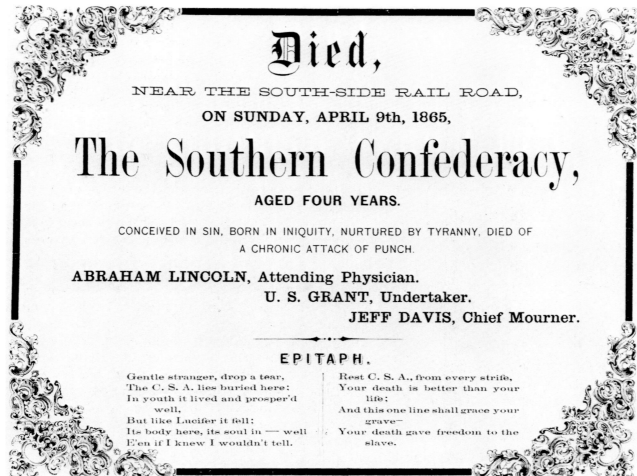

Died,

NEAR THE SOUTH-SIDE RAIL ROAD,

ON SUNDAY, APRIL 9th, 1865,

The Southern Confederacy,

AGED FOUR YEARS.

CONCEIVED IN SIN, BORN IN INIQUITY, NURTURED BY TYRANNY, DIED OF A CHRONIC ATTACK OF PUNCH.

ABRAHAM LINCOLN, Attending Physician.
U. S. GRANT, Undertaker.
JEFF DAVIS, Chief Mourner.

EPITAPH.

Gentle stranger, drop a tear,
The C. S. A. lies buried here:
In youth it lived and prosper'd
well,
But like Lucifer it fell;
Its body here, its soul in — well
E'en if I knew I wouldn't tell.

Rest C. S. A., from every strife,
Your death is better than your
life;
And this one line shall grace your
grave—
Your death gave freedom to the
slave.

Thus the South was occupied by armies like a conquered country and ruled by military law. Black voting rights were enforced at the point of a gun; 'carpetbaggers' poured into the South with their meager belongings packed in fabric satchels, some of them genuinely concerned with civil rights, more of them eager to profit at the expense of blacks and whites alike. The South struck back with the only weapon it had: terrorism. The ghastly white-sheeted Ku Klux Klan rode by night to murder and suppress the black population.

Lincoln had also said in his second inaugural that 'every drop of blood drawn with the lash, shall be paid by another drawn with the sword,' and so it had been. The Thirteenth Amendment to the Constitution, ratified in 1865, officially abolished slavery for good. However, by 1877, when the last Federal troops were withdrawn from the South, the Radical Republicans had died out and the government thereafter abandoned blacks to the mercies of their former slavemasters.

The Civil War accomplished other things less equivocally. It represented the final ascendancy of the Federal government over the power of the states (although the old warhorse of states' rights would be ridden for another hundred years in defense of segregation). The war also ensured Eastern industrial and economic superiority, making it still harder for the South to diversify its anachronistic agrarian economy. And it confirmed the importance and continued expansion of the railroads, marking the rise of a ruthless generation of 'robber barons' who would amass an unprecedented concentration of wealth and power.

The destinies of the leading figures took them down various paths, but for nearly all who participated in it, the war was the central experience of their lives. Ulysses S Grant became a popular but unfortunate president of the United States, presiding haplessly over the most corrupt administration in history. Robert E Lee became president of a Virginia college that would be renamed Washington and Lee in his honor, where misbehaving students dreaded facing him in his office. After Appomattox, Lee and Grant met one more time, in the White House, for political and economic discussions. In an effort to break the ice during a discussion about railroads, Grant joked that they used to tear them up rather than build them. Lee was not amused.

Grant died of throat cancer – the result of years of cigar smoking – in July 1885, a few days after finishing his extraordinary war memoirs. Lee died in October 1870 of a long-standing heart ailment; his last words were 'Strike the tents.' J E Johnston had surrendered his army to Sherman a few days after Appomattox. With a certain cynical irony, fate arranged for Johnston to die of pneumonia contracted at Sherman's rainy funeral. In 1866 Sherman had taken over from Grant as General in Chief of the Army; from that position he oversaw the last of the Indian Wars in the West. One of his associates was Phil Sheridan, who summed up their mutual policy in the phrase 'The only good Indian is a dead Indian.' Sheridan's brother-in-law, George Armstrong Custer, also fought the Indians with his old bravado until, at Little Big Horn, he finally rode into a tight situation he could not get out of. The likable if disastrous Ambrose E Burnside was three times elected governor of Rhode Island and thereafter became a United States senator.

Black people remained for a long and tragic century at the center of the social, legal, and political agenda of the South. The war had barely made blacks citizens and voters. In the decades to come, by a combination of enforced segregation, denial of voting rights, lynching, and terrorism – and with the co-operation of the US Government – the South disenfranchised and virtually re-enslaved them.

At last, when the dream of full citizenship began to be realized, the Civil War was the foundation on which the Civil Rights movement rested. Only then did the truth which the Declaration of Independence had called self-evident 200 years before begin to reveal its full meaning and power: 'All men are created equal.'

Left: *Jefferson Davis in prison after his capture by the 4th Michigan Cavalry on 10 May 1865.*

Below: *Andrew Johnson's impeachment committee.*

Above: Memento Mori.

Following page: *Reconstruction: Federal troops occupy New Orleans.*

Right: *The Freedmen's Bureau in Tennessee, 1866, from a contemporary woodcut.*

205

Quakers 9

raiding: shipping 166; supplies 50, 84, 156, 161
railroads 24, 59n, 118, 162, *162-63*; defense *83*; destruction *75*, 82-3, 98, 102, 156, 163, 164, *176*, *187*, 196
Reconstruction 202-03, *205, 206*
recruitment *21*, 156
Reynolds, John 110, 122
Richmond, campaign(s) for 44, 48-9, 72, 134, 138, 148, 162, 168; fall of *189*, 196
'Rock of Chickamauga' *see* George Thomas
Rosecrans, William S 78, 107, *118*, 118-22, *121, 126*, 156

St Louis USS *37*
Savage's Station, battle of 50
Savannah, occupation 190, *193, 194-5*
Schofield, John 162, 164, 180
Scott, Winfield 16, *23. 30*, 30, *31*, 31
scouts 38, 82, 84, 110, 121. *See also* intelligence
secession 9, 13, *14*, 14
Seminary Ridge *see* Gettysburg
Semmes, Raphael *166*, 166
Seven Days' Battles 50
Seven Pines *see* Fair Oaks
Sewall's Point (VA), battle of 20
Seward, William 16, 116, 130
Sharpsburg, *see* Antietam
sharpshooters 74, *123, 151*
Shenadoah Valley campaign 174, 176. *See also* Union Army, Peninsular Campaign
Sheridan, Philip 84, *135. 136*, 148, 174, *188*, 196, 198, 204; leadership *175*, 176, *189*

Sherman, William T 60, *61*, 98, 100, 102, 126, 129, *136*, 136, *157*, 161, 180, *188, 191*, 204; 'March to the Sea' *176*, 190 (*map 190*); taking of Atlanta 162-64
Shiloh, battle of *60-1*, 62, *62-3, 64-5*, 156
Sickles, Daniel 91, 111
Sigel, Franz 38, *59*, 136, 172
slavery *8*, 8, 9; abolition 203; escape from *10*; and politics *12*, 12-13, 70; and principles of equality/democracy 9, 131; and secession 14. *See also* blacks
Smith, William F 168
Snodgrass Hill 122
South: devastation *see* Union Army strategy; economy 88; occupation 206; refugees *32*; sectionalist sentiment 9, and rioting 20 *see also* Confederacy; Reconstruction; secession
South Carolina *193*; as first state to secede 14. *See also* Charleston
Spotsylvania 138; battle of 142, *142-43*, 144. *See also* Bloody Angle
Stanton, Edwin 116
states, border 20, 32; *See also* territories
states' rights, and seccession 9
Stephens, Alexander 88
Stoneman, George 90
Stones River, battle of 78
Stonewall Jackson USS 81
Stoughton, Edwin 82
Streight, Abel 156, *157*
Stuart, J E B 50, 82, 84, *85*, 90, 91, 94, 95, 107, *149*; death 148
Sturgis, S D 161
Sumner, Edwin 70

supplies 102, 126, 174; captured 161; centers 98; and Confederate military 88; destruction 55. *See also* raiding, Union Army strategy
Supreme Court: Dred Scott decision 11
Swift Run Gap 45

Tennessee 37, 78, 160; Chattanoog/ Chickamauga 118-22; Pittsburg Landing 60; Union victory in 62
Tennessee CSS 178, *181*
territories: expansion and slavery 9, 11, 13
Thomas, George H 32, 119, 120, 121, 122, *126*, 126, 129, *136*, 162, 164, 180, *182*, 186
troop movements: forced/night marches *45*; by rail *0*, 24, 196; by ship 54, 60
torpedoes *see* mines

Uncle Tom's Cabin 9, 9, 11
Underground Railroad *10*, 11
Union: civilian attitude to war 24, 38-9; flag 120
Union Army *26*, *78, 94-5, 165, 182-83*, 196; disorganization/dissension of 62, 72, 148; Irish Brigade 70; *See also specific armies*; draft; officers; volunteers
Union Army military strategy 24, 90, 134; at Antietam 70; Bull Run 54-7; Chattanooga: breaking/relieving siege 126, 129; Confederate supplies, destruction of/raiding countryside 161, 174, 176, 190, *190-91, 193*; Gettysburg 111, 114; ineptness/ confusion 72, 74, 122; and Peninsular Campaigns *4-5*, 44-6, 48-50;

Richmond, capture of 152, 168; Southern invasion *35*, 35, *36-7*, 37, 60, *88* (Vicksburg 98, 100, *100-01*, 102); unified strategy 136; withdrawal 91, 94-5, 119. *See also* armaments; engineering, naval warfare.
United States Army: military policy 16; officer conflict 22
Upton, Emory 142

Vallandigham, Clement *117*, 117
Van Dorn, Earl 38
Varuna USS 81
Vicksburg 98, 100, siege *76-7, 97, 98, 99, 100, 101*, 102-3, 102-03, *103*
Virginia CSS *see* Merrimack
Virginia Wilderness, battle of 138, *139, 140*
volunteers *15, 20*, 20, 22, 24. *See also* recruitment

Wallace, Lew 62, 172
Warren, Gouverneur 111
Washington, D C: protection of 20, *30*; raid on 172, *173*
Welles, Gideon 40
West Virginia, creation of 20
White Oak Swamp, battle of 50
Whitman, Walt 24
Wilderness *see* Virginia
Winchester (VA) 46, *49*, 174, 176; occupation 44
Wood, Thomas J 122
Worden, Lorimer 41

Yorktown *48*, 48-9

Zollicoffer, Felix 32
Zouaves *27, 154*

Picture Credits

Anne S. K. Brown Military Collection, Brown University: 1, 2-3, 4-5, 22(both), 23(top), 24(top), 26, 27, 30(left), 33(top), 36-37, 37, 39(bottom), 46, 47(top), 49(bottom), 51(top), 54-55, 59(top), 67(both),72(bottom), 73, 79(right), 82, 83(bottom), 87(both), 90, 94, 96(both),97, 98, 99(top), 100-01, 106-07, 108(bottom), 109, 112-113, 115(bottom), 120(top left), 121, 124-25, 128top), 134(top), 136, 137, 149(bottom), 150, 154(top left 2), 175, 177(bottom), 181(top), 182-83(both), 184-85, 188(both), 190, 191(top), 196(bottom).
The Bettmann Archive Inc.: 6-7, 48(left), 51(bottom), 63(bottom), 80(top left), 84, 85, 86, 99(bottom), 101, 102-03(top), 103, 122, 123(top), 126, 127(top), 141, 146-7, 149(top), 153(bottom), 154-55, 156, 157(right), 160, 160-61, 168, 170-71, 173(bottom), 178(right), 179, 180, 198(both), 199(both), 205(both), 206.
Bison Picture Library: 17(top), 19, 23(bottom), 26-27, 28-29, 31, 34-35, 35(bottom), 42(both), 43(both), 49(top), 52-53, 56-57, 60-61, 62-63, 64-65, 66, 68(both), 76-77, 80(both), 83(top), 102-03(bottom), 104-05, 108-09, 120(top right & bottom), 127(bottom), 128(bottom), 132-33, 135, 151, 152, 154(bottom left), 158-59, 176, 177(top), 178(left 2) 189(both), 192.
Chicago Historical Society: 17(bottom right), 55(bottom), 70, 71(top), 157(left), 197(bottom).
Cincinnati Art Museum: 10(bottom).
John Hay Library, Brown University: 12(top), 116, 202(bottom).
Rutherford B. Hayes Presidential Center: 20(bottom right), 24(bottom), 32, 47(bottom), 80(top right), 123(bottom), 134(bottom), 139(bottom).

Library of Congress: 8(both), 9(top 2), 10(top), 12(bottom), 13(all 3), 14(both), 15(top right & bottom), 16, 17(bottom left), 20(top & bottom left), 21(both), 25(top), 32-33, 36, 38-39, 39(top), 44-45, 45(bottom), 48(right), 50-51, 58-59, 63(top), 71(bottom), 79(both left), 88(top), 91, 107, 110-11(all 3), 114-15, 115(top), 117(both), 118, 130, 138, 139(top), 140(both), 144, 148, 162-63(both), 164, 165(top), 166, 169(both), 172-73, 173(top), 174, 186, 187(both), 190-91, 193(top), 194-95, 196(top), 197(top), 203(all 3), 204(both).
Louis A. Warren Lincoln Library & Museum: 69, 202(top).
The Metropolitan Museum of Art: 11
Museum of the Confederacy: 18(both), 72(top), 75(top), 92-93, 94-95, 153(top).
National Archives: 45(top), 130-31, 200-01.
National Portrait Gallery, Smithsonian Institution: 61.
New York Historical Society: 9(bottom).
New York Public Library: 55(top), 75(bottom), 142-43, 167(top).
Smith & Wesson: 79(top).
Springfield Armory NHS Photographic Collection: 129(all 3), 165(bottom).
U.S. Army: 78
Beverley R. Robinson Collection, U.S. Naval Academy Museum: 100
U.S. Naval Historical Center: 40, 166-67.
U.S. Navy: 81, 88(Bottom), 181(bottom), 193(bottom).
Virginia Military Institute: 25(bottom), 74, 118-19.
Virginia State Library: 15(top left), 30(right), 40-41, 145.

Acknowledgments

The author and publisher would like to thank the following people who helped in the preparation of this book: Adrian Hodgkins, who designed it; Robin L. Sommer, who edited it; Janet York, who did the picture research; and Cynthia Klein, who prepared the index.